Black and White Styles in Conflict

Thomas Kochman

Black and White Styles in Conflict

The University of Chicago Press
Chicago and London

THOMAS KOCHMAN is professor of communi-
cations and theater at the University of Illinois,
Circle Campus.

The University of Chicago Press, Chicago 60637
The University of Chicago Press, Ltd., London

© 1981 by The University of Chicago
All rights reserved. Published 1981
Paperback edition 1983
Printed in the United States of America

91 92 93 94 95 96   11 10 9 8 7

Library of Congress Cataloging in Publication Data

Kochman, Thomas.
  Black and white styles in conflict.

  Bibliography: p.
  Includes index.
  1. United States—Race relations.   2. Afro-Americans—
Communication.   3. Intercultural communication.   I. Title.
E185.615.K57   305.8′00973   81-3405
ISBN 0-226-44954-8 (cloth)
        0-226-44955-6 (paper)   AACR2

Contents

Acknowledgments

Many people have given generously of their time and knowledge to make this a better book. For critical reviews of an earlier version of the manuscript or portions of it, I wish to thank Roger Abrahams, Dell Hymes, Joan Foster McCarty, Stan Newman, Bruce Spivey, and John Szwed. For a critical reading of the present manuscript or various chapters I wish to thank Larry Fisher, Allen Harris, and Stan Newman. For being generally on call to give me critical reaction when I needed it, I am especially grateful to Allen Harris, Grace Holt, Joan Foster McCarty, and Stan Newman.

For valuable editorial help with portions of the manuscript, I wish to thank Isabel Grossner and Carolyn Mullins. For helpful editorial advice and criticism I also wish to thank Anthony Graham-White and Frank Williams.

I also owe a great debt of thanks to my students, usually the first group to respond critically to my views about cultural differences between blacks and whites. They also provided me with examples from their own experience that I have used extensively for both documentation and illustration throughout the book.

For her unflagging good will and care in typing the manuscript, I wish to thank Marquita Hampton.

My deepest thanks go to my wife Alexandra, whose unwavering support and encouragement sustained me spiritually through the entire project. I also wish to thank my daughters Adrienne and Switlana for their support.

Introduction

I don't understand you.
I don't know who you are.

Maxim Gorky, *Enemies*

My research on black language and culture began in the summer of 1966 when I spent a week in the black community in the Bronx, New York, putting together a glossary of black vernacular vocabulary. This was to fulfill an assignment for a summer institute on the "disadvantaged," as blacks and members of other minority groups were then called. Attendance at the institute marked the end of five years of teaching junior high school English in New York City and the beginning of college teaching in Chicago.

My research intensified when the director of Chicago's Center for Inner City Studies asked me to teach a graduate course on black language. It was at that point that I discovered how little material on black language and culture had been published. Consequently, what I had to distribute to that first class was embarrassingly meager in proportion to the wealth of information that the students knew themselves or knew existed within the community. The need to remedy this disparity was apparent, both to overcome the years of general neglect on the subject and, most pressing from a personal standpoint, to make both myself and the course respectable.

These goals were accomplished with the help of students who gathered and provided information and helped me gain access to the community to gather information myself. The material that was obtained through this process—each class becoming a resource for the next—established the curriculum of the course. The material also eventually reached well beyond the center, serving both graduating students and colleagues who were to start similar courses at other universities. Much of it was also published in a collection I edited (Kochman 1972). The book included articles by students, colleagues at the center, myself, and other researchers who had been doing similar fieldwork elsewhere. It appropriately reflected the ferment, collaboration, and cross-fertilization of this period.

This was also a period that contributed much to my own political education. Issues emerged that transcended the usual academic considerations: whether the course was a good course or I a good teacher or researcher. One such issue was black self-determination. This included blacks assuming traditionally white-held positions, such as in education, that impinged directly on black community life. Consequently it also extended to white instructors teaching black courses. I was never asked outright to step aside, but the signs coming from black students and colleagues were clear and compelling. Therefore I asked to step down, having overcome my initial reluctance to give up a course that I had come to be identified with and so thoroughly enjoyed. I also indicated my willingness to serve the center in ways in which my role as a white instructor would be less of a burden. Like so many whites working in black contexts at the time, my first thought was that the issue was simply a matter of being white or black. Unlike many of my white colleagues, however, I discovered that while being black or white was obviously relevant, the determining issue was then and has since been accountability: accepting a role that would fit within a black political program leading to emancipation from racism, social oppression, and cultural subordination. It also meant being sensitive to the needs of blacks and other minorities to assume greater self-determination over those areas that directly affected their lives.

While teaching at the center, I had already indicated that my own sensibilities and goals for social change—humanism, cultural pluralism, social egalitarianism—would fit well into a program leading to the emancipation of blacks and other socially oppressed minorities. But perhaps more important, in agreeing to step aside, I demonstrated my willingness to accept black leadership in this effort. Consequently, when the center staff was given a contract to provide consultants to work with the black community in Dayton, Ohio, under a Model Cities Education grant, I was asked to participate. Furthermore, when I went to the University of Illinois in 1970, it was a black colleague who was instrumental in bringing me there, blacks in key administrative positions who had determinative votes in hiring me, and black students who ultimately confirmed my appointment.

Today I demonstrate accountability as a matter of course. When I meet minority students in my classes for the first time, I know that where I stand with respect to issues and my personal philosophy will be as important to them as what I know about their language and culture. I also know that I need to indicate where I am going with the information. Consequently information is presented not just as an interesting set of facts but for the sake of argument. Argument in turn is presented for the sake of persuasion, and persuasion for the sake of social change. It is because I use information in this way that I continue to receive the support and cooperation of blacks. In my opinion, the days are gone when anthropologists could work with minority groups simply to demonstrate the methods and procedures of their discipline or to obtain interesting comparative data. If anthropologists are to work with minority groups today, they will be able to serve anthropology and their own career goals only insofar as these are compatible with the social needs and goals of the minority groups with whom they work.

My approach in collecting and analyzing the information presented here is ethnographic. Ethnography as a form of inquiry employs two basic principles. One is that the investigator collecting the information be on the scene as a participant and observer. This is premised on the well-founded view among linguists and anthropologists that the patterns of language and culture are best seen and understood within the contexts in which they originate and develop or are in regular use. The other principle is that the description of performances that are part of a cultural scene should attend to meanings that the principal actors themselves give to what is going on (see Hymes 1972, p. 64). These meanings—if properly attended to by the ethnographer—should reveal the community norms, operating principles, strategies, and values that guide the production and interpretation of performances such as speech behavior (Bauman and Sherzer 1974), p. 7).

During the course of this study, however, I was not merely a participant and observer. More often than not, I was a principal interactant, one whose own middle-class cultural background was a relevant operational frame of reference throughout. In fact, my initial experience of unaccustomed reactions by blacks to my behavior in the contexts in which I was working, together with an analysis of my own variant reactions to black presentations, led me to suppose that more was going on than could be attributed to factors of caste and class alone. This led me to look at black and white interactions in an attempt to discover what participants were seeing in each other's behavior that prompted them to react as they did. The kinds of behaviors that seemed to be causing the difficulty, and what blacks and whites were saying about these behaviors, began to repeat themselves. Eventually patterns began to emerge that did not depend on the specific individuals present or on the nature of the agenda of the encounter. These patterns led me to conclude that the points of view were cultural and to explore further and attempt to reconstruct the cultural factors that shaped the patterns and attitudes that blacks and whites brought with them to the communication situation.

The descriptions offered here are not complete. Consequently they do not entirely satisfy the goal of ethnographic descriptions: that such descriptions be sufficiently detailed to enable those unfamiliar with a culture to behave and to interpret behavior in ways that members of the culture would consider appropriate (Frake 1964, p. 112). Rather, I have selected those patterns of behavior, or elements within patterns, and mapped black and white cognitive territory, to reveal or clarify the cultural reasons for a communication difficulty. In some measure, then, my method presumes that readers will be able to draw upon their own interracial experiences, and I hope they will reconsider their original interpretations of these experiences. I do not know how useful this book will be to those who have no experiential frame of reference into which the analyses can be fit. I think enough people will have one, however, to make this book generally useful.

There are many ways in which I have personally benefited from my association with blacks over the years. I speak not only of the assistance that I received in my work but of the friendships that I have made and the ways in which my own value system has been affected. Black culture has given me a powerful appreciation of qualities and concerns that my own white middle-class culture tends to downgrade: individual self-assertion and self-expression, spiritual well-being, spontaneity and emotional expressiveness, personal (as opposed to status) orientation, individual distinctiveness, forthrightness, cameraderie, and community. Black affirmation of these qualities in myself has strengthened them, increased my estimation of them, and enriched my life considerably in the process of doing so.

One

Black Culture

Black and white cultural differences are generally ignored when attempts are made to understand how and why black and white communication fails.

One reason for this is that cultural differences play a covert role in the communication process. When blacks and whites interact in public meetings, their agenda does not typically include a discussion of the way they are interpreting each other's behavior, the reasons they are interpreting it as they do, or the way they are expecting the meeting to evolve. Thus, unless there are reasons to think otherwise, blacks and whites at such gatherings will assume that the meanings they are assigning to all of these matters are the same and, therefore, that the motives they are ascribing to each other—based on this assumption—are also justified.

Also, given the nature of the issues about which whites and blacks typically interact in public, cultural differences will probably not be the only reason interracial communication has failed. Since these other reasons can also serve to account for why things went wrong and are also more readily identifiable, blacks and whites will not feel compelled to search beyond them for other possible causes.

Of course the chief reason cultural differences are ignored is that blacks and whites assume they are operating according to identical speech and cultural conventions and that these are the conventions the socially dominant white group has established as standard. This assumption—besides adding to the disruptive capacity of cultural differences—speaks to the general public failure to recognize that black norms and conventions in these areas differ from those of whites. It is also the chief obstacle to considering how they differ.

A major share of responsibility for the general view that blacks have no distinctive culture must be carried by social scientists who, barring a few exceptions, have promoted the view that African culture was all but destroyed by slavery. Herskovits ([1941] 1958, p. 1), one of the notable exceptions here, called such a view a myth. Yet as recently as 1963, Glazer would write, "The Negro is only an American and nothing else. He has no values and culture to guard and protect" (Glazer and Moynihan 1963, p. 53). Indeed in 1967, in putting together material for a course on black language, I found little published on the subject and only a handful of language scholars willing to concede that such a distinct phenomenon as black language existed. The consequence of viewing blacks without their own language or culture was to see their different behavior as distortions of white behavior, due to their social distance from the white mainstream where such behavior was regularly in use, or as pathological responses to the oppressive forces of caste and class (Stewart 1974, pp. 1–2). The distinctive grammatical patterns of blacks were seen not as governed by their own set of rules but as a random collection of mistakes. No search for an underlying structure to black behavior was undertaken, because none was presumed to exist.

Even when black behavior was not categorized as pathological or as a distortion of white behavior, the absence of a black cultural frame of reference still resulted only in social explanations of black behavior, which, because they were *exclusively* social, were often also incomplete. Thus David Wolf (1972, p. 41) explained the spectacular exhibitionism that marks black playing style in basketball as a means by which impoverished black youths could rise above the "drabness and anonymity of their lives." This social view is not necessarily false, taking into account as it does the psychological need of individuals for status among their peers. But it is not the whole truth, for it does not account for the *style* of the black response, the flair or, as Jeff Greenfield (1975, p. 170) called it, the "liquid grace" that characterizes black basketball. Oppressive social conditions may account more or less satisfactorily for playing with a punishing drive and intensity. But as Paul Carter Harrison (1972, pp. 25–26) and Roger Abrahams (1976, pp. 82–92) have each pointed out, the stylistic aspects of black performances need to be viewed against more broadly conceived aesthetic notions within the culture. There is a difference between simply playing aggressively and demonstrating personal power through the activation of vital and expressive images (Harrison 1972, pp. 32–34).

Likewise, a failure to recognize the substance or scope of expressiveness in black culture led one writer to attribute the "new expressiveness" in sports like football to the influence of Martha Graham and to see it simply as a fad, likely to disappear in the near future, "retained only in film clips or enshrined in some 1980's version of 'That's Entertainment'" (McDowell 1976, p. 16). Those who know the cultural function and value of expressive behavior for blacks also know that, if blacks have anything to say about it, this forecast simply will not materialize.

Blacks have been hurt by the general failure to recognize the distinctiveness of black culture in other ways: for example, on standardized psychological tests. Thus Thomas Pettigrew (1964, p. 19) reported that, when the Minnesota Multiphasic Inventory (MMPI) was administered to black and white Alabama jail prisoners and Wisconsin working-class veterans with tuberculosis, black males scored higher than whites on the test's "measure of femininity" because they agreed more often with such "feminine" choices as "I would like to be a singer" and "I think that I feel more intensely than most people do." But as Erik

Erikson noted (1968, p. 306), "to be a singer and to feel intensely may be facets of a masculine ideal gladly admitted if you grew up in a southern Negro community (or for that matter, in Naples)."

The test designers interpreted these choices as "feminine" because they used only dominant white cultural norms as reference. Thus, singing, like ballet dancing, was an appropriate desire for females in white culture, but not for males. Likewise, only females were permitted to give full expression to their feelings. As Philip Slater put it (1976, p. 3), about the only emotion males were permitted to show was anger, which was about the only emotion females were *not* permitted to show. But intense feeling and emotional expressiveness are not the only characteristics over whose sexual classification blacks and whites would disagree. Diane Lewis, for example, has posited a range of behavioral traits that whites would consider "masculine" or "feminine" but blacks would consider common to both sexes. These are aggressiveness, independence, self-confidence, nonconformity, sexual assertiveness, nurturance, emotional expressiveness, and focus on personal relationships. Whites would consider the first five traits "masculine" and the last three as "feminine" (Lewis 1975, p. 230).

Blacks have also been hurt by the failure to recognize distinctively black *racial* attributes. Thus Stanley Garn and Diane Clark point out that, if dimensional differences between blacks and whites are not taken into account and only white standards for normal growth and development are used as reference, problems will arise when nutritional assessments of black individuals are made. For example, based on surveys of large numbers of blacks and whites, Garn and Clark indicate that blacks at birth are smaller than whites in weight and length and that these birth differences hold even after income-matching. On the other hand, from the age of two through fourteen, black males and females are taller than their white cohorts. They conclude that if only white standards are used, those blacks at birth who are normal by black standards may be incorrectly assessed as nutritionally deficient. More serious, if only white standards are used for blacks during the age period two to fourteen, "some proportion of black children actually at nutritional risk will then be improperly judged satisfactory or normal, to their long-term disadvantage" (Garn and Clark 1976, pp. 262–64).

It is perhaps ironic that the kind of public discussion and scholarly inquiries needed to challenge the incorrect and often pejorative characterization of black behavior should be hampered by efforts originally aimed at relieving blacks and other minority groups of the stigma the public has attached to their different cultural behavior. For example, there still exists a social etiquette that considers it impolite to discuss minority-group differences in public. This rule emerged over a period when such differences were regularly used as evidence of minority-group inferiority. To resist this implication, minority-group members felt it necessary to divert attention away from ways in which they were distinctive. This included generally working to prevent discussion of differences. Some even went so far as to deny that they existed. Liberal-minded whites cooperated with minorities in these efforts, since they shared the general view that these differences were signs of minority-group inferiority. Consequently, they felt that their public discussion would be, as Joan and Stephen Baratz put it, tantamount to discussing a hunchback's hump with him (1972, p. 13).

The problem with this strategy is that it left the public view of minority-group differences intact, working equally against those who would talk about them to challenge incorrect and often negative interpretations and those who would use them to document minority-group inferiority. By and large, members of minority groups today must still confront a public view that sees their distinctive racial, cultural, and linguistic features as a source of public embarrassment.

Since the late 1960s many blacks and other minority-group members—especially younger people—have challenged this negative view of minority-group behavior, thereby forcing some segments of the public, like the scholastic establishment, to modify some of its earlier attitudes and policies. Where schools throughout the mid-1960s were uniformly committed to the eradication of black language patterns, they are now willing to acknowledge that these have some functional value for blacks when used within the context of their own community. This acknowledgment became formally recognized by the National Council of Teachers of English when they endorsed the language statement of their Committee on College Composition and Communication on "Students' Right to Their Own Language." Consequently schools, by and large, have been given the charge to move toward a more "bidialectal" approach to language teaching, one in which standard (white) English would become an addition, not a replacement.

The Bilingual Education Act expanded the idea of students' right to their own language to their right to be educated in their own language, if their command of English was insufficient for them to learn on a par with native English-speaking students in classrooms where only English was spoken. While obviously conceived as a transition *to* an English program, in effect, bilingual education also strengthens students' abilities to communicate in their own language, if that is the language in which it has been determined that they can learn more effectively. The social significance of this development, however unintentional, is that public schools—perhaps for the first time on a national scale—have become actively engaged in *maintaining* the native language of ethnic minority groups.

From the standpoint of social *parity,* these gains of minorities in the area of language do not amount to that much of a concession by the dominant social group, in that they do not change existing patterns of social accommodation. Bidialectalism and bilingualism, as presently defined, still expect minority students to learn and use the speech patterns of the dominant group in the wider society in the same way as before. Moreover, the concession of bidialectalism to native dialect maintenance is a negative one: it agrees not to attempt to eradicate it, but it does nothing to support or encourage its use or development.

Nonetheless, the recognition that students have language rights has led schools to assume responsibility for providing transitions between the native language of the student and that of the school. This has led to increased interest in educational research on language differences, functional as well as structural (see, e.g., Aarons, Gordon, and Stewart 1969; and Cazden, John, and Hymes 1972). It has also prompted scholastics to work to develop pedagogical strategies that will take these differences into account.

The issues involving cultural differences are much the same as those involving language differences. But they have not as yet had the same kind of impact, because contrasting cultural studies involving minorities have lagged behind similar language studies. Consequently it is relatively easy now to understand what bilingualism and bidialectalism are because the structures of the two languages or dialects have been identified, as have been, in some measure, their patterns of convergence and use. It is also possible to determine how speakers are being influenced as they move within and between the two systems in various social contexts. But how is the biculturalism or multiculturalism of individuals to be assessed? Without the contrasting cultural studies that would identify the cultural norms and patterns of the various contact groups, we are unable to tell.

The contrasting data provided in this book can be used to address the question of individual acculturation. This is because the different meanings that blacks and whites assign to their own and each other's behavior in effect reflect black and white cultural perspectives, at least with respect to those patterns of behavior that cause communicative conflict. Since these perspectives identify ways in which the two cultures are different, they can be used to indicate the extent to which blacks and whites have become bicultural. When correlated with social data, they can be used to indicate which blacks and whites are more likely to become bicultural and even which aspects of black culture tend to become lost—or saved—as blacks move further into social contexts or areas governed by white cultural norms. For example, a long-standing question has been how "black" or "white" are the black middle class or, taking into account their respective ethnic backgrounds, how "ethnic" and "white" are the middle classes of other ethnic groups? Allen Harris, one of my black students, has noted that the problem with most media portrayals of black middle-class people is that their behavior is typically represented as either exactly like "community" inner-city blacks or exactly like white middle-class people. For most middle-class blacks, who have typically incorporated aspects of both cultures, both portrayals are inaccurate.

As used in this book, the terms *black* and *white* reflect cultural patterns and perspectives almost entirely. Specifically, *white* is intended to represent the cultural patterns and perspectives of the dominant social group, also called in other studies *white mainstream, white middle-class, Anglo, Anglo-American. Black* represents the ethnic patterns and perspectives of black "community" people, called elsewhere *ghetto blacks, inner-city blacks,* or *Afro-Americans.*

My confidence in the "whiteness" and "blackness" of those cultural patterns and perspectives is based upon the authority of those from whom the information was directly obtained and the representativeness of those who displayed such patterns in the contexts in which I was a participant and observer. It also comes from cultural descriptions by other field investigators both within and outside the United States. Some of the black patterns and perspectives described here have also been found among blacks in the Caribbean. These parallel observations reinforce the view that they are indeed *black* ethnic patterns and, with regard to their source, African influenced or derived.

Because the term *black* describes the patterns and perspectives of black "community" people, there are those who will argue that these are *class* as opposed to *cultural* patterns and perspectives. I would reject that view, even though I acknowledge, following Herskovits ([1941] 1958, p. xxvi), that the black cultural perspective will be more prevalent among blacks at a lower socio-economic level than among middle- or upper-income blacks. But that is only to recognize, along with Charles Valentine (1968, p. 25), that "ethnic identity and subcultural distinctness of all or many minorities are greatest for group members who are poor." Thus, just as poor first-generation Irish, Italian, Jewish, or Ukrainian groups are likely to be more "ethnic" than their third-generation middle-class counterparts, so would poor blacks be more "ethnic" than their black middle-class counterparts whose social networks, or level of education, has brought them more within the sphere of influence of dominant white cultural norms and values. That "community" blacks, even after several generations, should retain their original ethnic patterns and perspectives simply speaks to the extent to which racial segregation has kept the black rural and urban community culturally insular.

This is not to deny that lower-income blacks—or for that matter whites—will have patterns of behavior or perspectives that are class derived or related. It is simply to say that if a pattern or perspective is to be called class related, it must be one that arises from a class or colonial situation, such as those that Albert

Memmi has described for both colonizers as well as colonized (1965, passim). It should not be labeled "class" simply because it is found most distinctly among the poor.

Class-related perspectives regularly surface among black, Latino, and white students. For example, one assignment that I give asks students to go into more expensive department stores to pretend to buy something in order to investigate speech patterns. In doing so they often find themselves receiving a great deal of personal attention from the sales clerks. Most of the black and Latino students in the class attribute part of the reason for such attentiveness to the employees' assumption that they are going to steal something. This never occurs to the white middle-class students, who see such personal attention as simply reflecting the kind of service one gets at the better stores and, of course, the eagerness of the sales clerks to make a sale. The opposing views of the black and Latino students on one hand and the white students on the other I would consider class-related conceptions.

While class-related views such as these will generally not be considered here, occasionally a view with a cultural origin and function will also have a social function. Such a social function will be taken into account. An example can be found in the different etiquettes of blacks and whites on the propriety of using direct questions to obtain personal information. The basis for this etiquette is cultural, as I point out in chapter 6. But it acquires social significance from the different degrees of social vulnerability that blacks and whites experience in American society.

Two

Classroom Modalities

In November 1914, Monroe Trotter, an educator and equal rights activist, led a black delegation to the White House to renew the protest against the segregation of federal employees that had become widespread for the first time during Woodrow Wilson's administration. President Wilson indicated that the intention of such segregation was to avoid friction between black and white clerks. Trotter disputed this, saying that white and black clerks had been working together for fifty years in peace, harmony, and friendliness and that it was only after Wilson's inauguration that segregation was to a drastic degree introduced in the Treasury and Postal Departments by Wilson's appointees. Trotter's rebuttal brought about the following exchange:

Wilson: If this organization is ever to have another hearing before me it must have another spokesman. Your manner offends me.

Trotter: In what way?

Wilson: Your tone, with its background of passion.

Trotter: But I have no passion in me, Mr. President, you are entirely mistaken; you misinterpret my earnestness for passion. ["Mr. Trotter and Mr. Wilson" 1915, pp. 119–20]

In another, more recent meeting that I attended, between community representatives and university faculty, members of each group were similarly distracted from the issue—in this case a proposal for a graduate study program in urban education—because of the way disagreements were expressed. For example, the faculty felt that the behavior of the community representatives did not meet appropriate requirements for rational discussion. One faculty member characterized the heated session as a "Baptist revival meeting." Another called it a "pep rally." The community representatives considered the behavior of the faculty lacking in "sincerity" and "honest conviction." Some considered it "devious."

This meeting and the earlier encounter between Trotter and Wilson are indicative of what often happens when blacks and whites engage each other in public debate about an issue; they are divided not only over content—the issue itself—but, more fundamentally, over process: how disagreement on an issue is to be appropriately handled.

I think we can account for the different views of blacks and whites on how to address an issue in public properly. This account will consider the meaning and value that blacks and whites attach to their own and to each other's behavior. It will also consider more fundamental aspects of black and white culture and communication in order to explain why the patterns should have such meanings and values.

The information for this chapter comes partly from personal experiences in meetings such as those cited above: my own and those reported to me by others or recorded in the literature. Principally, the information comes from my own classes, which over the years have typically drawn a heavy enrollment of both black and white students. These classes have given me numerous opportunities to observe the different patterns of behavior that blacks and whites display in such contexts, to inquire about their meaning and value, and to reflect upon their larger social and cultural significance.

Modes of Behavior

The modes of behavior that blacks and whites consider appropriate for engaging in public debate on an issue differ in their stance and level of spiritual intensity. The black mode—that of black community people—is high-keyed: animated, interpersonal, and confrontational. The white mode—that of the middle class—is relatively low-keyed: dispassionate, impersonal, and non-challenging. The first is characteristic of involvement; it is heated, loud, and generates affect. The second is characteristic of detachment and is cool, quiet, and without affect.

Argument and Discussion

Blacks and whites both classify the black mode as argument. But this agreement on classification is misleading, concealing as it does deeper formal and functional differences.

For example, blacks distinguish between argument used to debate a difference of opinion and argument used to ventilate anger and hostility. Formally both modes consist of affect and dynamic opposition; however, this resemblance is only superficial. In the first form of argument—for persuasion—the affect shown is expressive of debaters' relation to their material. Its presence indicates that people are sincere and serious about what they are saying. On the other hand, the affect present in the form of argument that is a ventilation of anger and hostility is more intense; it is more passionate than earnest. It also emphasizes less a positive attitude toward one's material than a negative attitude toward one's opponent.

This same formal and functional distinction applies to dynamic opposition. In argument for persuasion, blacks assume a challenging stance with respect to their opponents. But blacks are not antagonists here. Rather, they are contenders cooperatively engaged in a process that hopes to test through challenge the validity of opposing ideas. Dynamic opposition within the framework of argument that is a ventilation of anger and hostility is again more intense than in persuasive argument. Opponents are viewed as antagonists, givers and receivers of abuse, not simply contenders engaged in a struggle to produce a more valid thought or idea.

Because the two kinds of argument function differently in black culture, blacks are also alert to those formal elements that distinguish them: not simply the presence of affect and dynamic opposition but the degree of their intensity and the direction of their focus.

Whites, on the other hand, fail to make these distinctions because argument for them functions only to ventilate anger and hostility. It does not function as a process of persuasion. For persuasion whites use discussion that is devoid of affect and dynamic opposition. Consequently whites feel that people are not engaging in persuasion when affect and dynamic opposition are present. The mere presence of affect and dynamic opposition, regardless of focus or intensity, is seen as the preliminary to a mode whose function is to ventilate anger and hostility. In their failure to make the same distinction as blacks, whites misinterpret black intentions, not believing that blacks are acting in good faith when they say they wish to resolve disagreement.

The negative attitude of whites toward argument as a process of persuasion is only partly influenced by the function of argument in their own culture. For even were they to be convinced that the black mode was intended to persuade and not to ventilate anger and hostility (and this conviction can come about after black and white students have interacted for a while) whites still regard the black argumentative mode as dysfunctional because of their view that reason and emotion work against each other; the presence of the latter militates against the operation of the former. This explains why discussion, the white mode for testing and validating ideas, is devoid of affect and why its presence, to whites, automatically renders any presentation less persuasive to the extent that affect is also present.

In discussion whites also hope to avoid dynamic opposition. This is because they see confrontation as leading to intransigence, a hardening of opposing viewpoints, with the result that neither opponent will listen to the other's viewpoint, regardless of its merit, let alone concede the possibility of its validity. Thus whites equate confrontation with conflict. Their goal is "openmindedness": flexibility in approach and the recognition that no one person has all the answers. To realize these aims, whites place their faith in a mode of intellectual engagement that weakens or eliminates those aspects of character or posture that they believe keep people's minds closed and make them otherwise unyielding.

Blacks do not believe that the presence of affect and dynamic opposition leads to intransigence. Quite the opposite: they often use formal argument as a means of testing their own views. Thus they speak their minds with the expectation that either their views or those of the opposition will be modified as a result of a successful challenge, a point against which one or the other opponent has no effective reply.

Struggle

Black and white concepts of intransigence derive from opposite views of the relevance of struggle in the persuasive process. Whites attempt to minimize dynamic opposition within the persuasive process because such confrontation, or struggle, is seen as divisive. Blacks, however, see such struggle as unifying or operating within, not outside, the persuasive process. It signifies caring about something enough to want to struggle for it. At the same time, blacks regard intransigence as a refusal to contend, a rejection of the struggle through which opposing ideas are tested and reconciliations are effected. It means, as my student Joan McCarty put it, "you'll stay your way, and I'll stay mine." The withholding of affect also has this meaning. As McCarty said, "when blacks are working hard to keep cool, it signals that the chasm between them is getting wider, not smaller."

Relation to Material

For blacks, the element of struggle is communicated primarily through dynamic opposition. But it is also conveyed by the way people relate to their material. Blacks present their views as advocates. They take a position and show that they care about this position. This stance is characteristic of the mode of predominantly oral cultures like that of present-day black community people and white society of an earlier era. In the latter society, as Walter Ong has pointed out, a scholar was taught to defend a position he had taken or to attack the position of another. The orator's stance, passionate involvement in his material and a feeling that there was an adversary at large, was standard equipment provided by formal education for man's confrontation with the world (Ong 1967, p. 225). This perspective survives in such general expressions as "taking a stand," which still retains its positive connotation in white usage.

Present-day whites relate to their material as spokesmen, not advocates. This is because they believe that the truth or other merits of an idea are intrinsic to the idea itself. How deeply a person cares about or believes in the idea is considered irrelevant to its fundamental value. The truth of the matter is in the matter. This view—the separation of truth and belief—is heavily influenced by what whites understand of the scientific method, where the goal is to achieve a stance of neutral objectivity with regard to the truth that is "out there": a truth that is not to be possessed or created but, rather, discovered. Whites believe that caring about one's own ideas, like the infatuation of scientists with their own hypotheses, will make them less receptive to opposing ideas and consequently prevent them from discovering the real truth. Thus they are taught to present ideas as though the ideas had an objective life, existing independent of any person expressing them. This accounts for the impersonal mode of expression that whites use, which, along with the absence of affect and dynamic opposition, establishes the detached character of proceedings in which white cultural norms dominate.

Black community people do not strive for totally neutral objectivity. As Joan McCarty put it—herself a black teacher of black students—"I've personally found it difficult in my classes to get people just to discuss an issue. They invariably take sides. Sometimes being neutral is looked upon with disdain."

Roles and Responsibilities

Because blacks admit that they deal from a point of view, they are disinclined to believe whites who claim not to have a point of view, or who present their views in a manner that suggests that they do not themselves believe what they are saying. This is why they often accuse whites of being insincere.

But they have another reason to misinterpret (and distrust) the dispassionate and detached mode that whites use to engage in debate. It resembles the mode that blacks themselves use when they are *fronting:* that is, consciously suppressing what they truly feel or believe. As one black student put it, "That's when I'm lyin'." Fronting generally occurs in black/white encounters when blacks perceive a risk factor and they decide it would be more prudent to keep silent than to speak. As one black woman, Deloris Williams, said, "When in the minority, only a fool shows the anger that he feels."

Both conceptions underlie the way blacks initially interpret and respond to white reticence in the classroom. For example, they believe not that whites hold no position on an issue but, rather, that they are reluctant to reveal their position. Blacks' attitude toward white reticence or silence, consequently, depends upon their perception and assessment of the present risk factor for white students. If the majority of the class is black, they are likely to be sympathetic toward white silence, often being the silent minority themselves. But when the black/white student ratio is about 50:50, blacks are not inclined to interpret (or accept) white lack of participation as a reaction to a risk factor. Instead, it is viewed either as intransigence—a refusal to engage in the struggle through which opposing ideas are tested and validated—or as deviousness—an unwarranted concealment of what they really think and believe ("unwarranted" because the black students perceive no present risk factor). At this point blacks often comment, "How come black people are the only ones doing the talking?" Should whites still remain generally silent after this invitation to participate, blacks will either start to question individual white students directly or make deliberately provocative statements to goad whites into speaking. One black woman, becoming impatient with the wall of white silence, finally said that she thought white men "couldn't handle it sexually." She knew "by the way they walked and talked." Joan McCarty, who reported the incident, thought her remark was intended to get the white students to talk. But they still remained silent. The white men flushed, and the white women looked down at the floor. The black students stared at the white students, amazed that such a remark would go unanswered. Moreover, the black woman who made the remark indicated that, until she did get a response, she would just "go on talking."

White students are typically bewildered and chagrined when this happens, because they do not see their reticence or silence as intransigence or deviousness. One white female student said, "I hardly ever talk in class," thereby hoping to convince the black students that her passive, receptive posture was her *customary* mode of classroom behavior.

But whites resent being called upon to justify their silence. They do not consider talking in class something that can be demanded. It is, after all, their right to remain silent if they so choose, just as it is their right not to answer direct personal questions ("I don't see why I have to answer that"). Such questions are seen by white students as outside the boundaries of "class discussion."

Blacks, however, do not agree that silence is a right in this instance, since it runs directly counter to what they regard as obligatory behavior for engaging in debate. For ideas to be tested and validated, all parties must engage in the process. To refuse to participate, especially if one really disagrees with what has been said (silence signifies agreement) is "cheating." It withholds from the group an attitude that might cause the prevailing view to be modified, and is thus considered subversive of a process in which ideas are validated to the extent that the best thoughts of everyone have been entered and tested against each other.

Blacks also disagree with the white belief that probing into an individual's personal viewpoint is outside the boundaries of class discussion. This is because they feel that all views expressed and actions taken derive from a central set of core beliefs that cannot be other than personal. As Carolyn Rodgers put it, "ultimately a person's life-style is his point of view" (1972, p. 345). Consequently blacks often probe beyond a given statement to find out where a person is "coming from," in order to clarify the meaning and value of a particular behavior or attitude.

As a result I regularly outline, in my opening lecture on black and white racial, cultural, and speech differences, my personal position on such differences. My intention is to inform students that when I talk about differences, it is not with the idea of reinforcing existing prejudices against them. Without this clarification of where I stand, it would be difficult to continue discussing the subject, since differences have typically been used as evidence of biological or social group inferiority, and members of minority groups are particularly sensitive to the possibility that a discussion of ethnic differences will have these implications.

Certifying Knowledge

Blacks and whites also disagree on what establishes the authority of an idea. White students regard as authoritative ideas that have been published or otherwise certified by experts in the field. For blacks, the publication of an idea is not sufficient to establish its authority. Authoritative ideas are those whose truth value has been tested by the crucible of argument. These conceptions directly affect the different ways that blacks and whites define their role and responsibility when engaged in debate.

For example, whites debate an issue as impersonally as possible. Theses are advanced to the group as a whole. Those who agree or disagree with one thesis or another are expected to present their views in the same impersonal manner. Individuals are not directly addressed; ideas are. The relative merits of the ideas are assessed independently, with minimal regard to how they were presented or who introduced them into the discussion.

Blacks, however, debate issues by engaging those who initially advanced the thesis in personal argument. This is because they consider debate to be as much a contest between individuals as a test of opposing ideas. Because it is a contest, attention is also paid to performance, for winning the contest requires that one outperform one's opponents: outthink, outtalk, and outstyle them. It means being concerned with art as well as argument. Also because it is a contest, no third person may redirect its focus until the outcome has been decided. This usually occurs when one or the other contender is unable to come back with an effective reply. At that point other participants may enter the debate to test and develop the truth value of the opposing ideas further.

Blacks and whites define their roles and responsibilities in terms of these conceptions. For example, because white students consider an idea authoritative when it has been published, they see their role and responsibility as limited to presenting the idea and its source accurately and showing its relevance to the topic under consideration. They do not see themselves as personally responsible for the idea itself. Nor do they see that they must necessarily agree with the idea or have any personal position on it at all. On the other hand, blacks consider it essential for individuals to have personal positions on issues and assume full responsibility for arguing their validity. Otherwise, they feel that individuals would not care enough about truth or their own ideas to want to struggle for them. And without such struggle, the truth value of ideas cannot be ascertained.

Hence black and white debate on an issue usually produces the following scenario. White students make statements that they believe are authoritative by virtue of who said them and where they were published. Black students cast the statements into the framework of personal argument and challenge the white students directly on one or another point with which they disagree. Because the white students did not intend their statements to be put in the context of an argument, they see the challenge as inappropriate. Consequently they respond with "Don't ask me, ask McLuhan" or "You ought to be arguing with McLuhan; he was the one who said it." But this response is also a convenient escape because, not having thought about the validity of the idea as an idea, they have no intellectual basis from which to defend it.

The black students consider such responses irresponsible and evasive, a way to say things without allowing oneself to be held accountable for them. Thus, should white students continue to cite authorities in their presentations, blacks will say, "Never mind what McLuhan says. What do *you* say?" Only statements for which an individual will assume personal responsibility in argument are admissible in debate.

Turn-taking

Collisions between black and white students in the classroom are also caused by different procedures for turn-taking, or claiming the floor. The white classroom rule is to raise your hand, be recognized by the instructor, and take a turn in the order in which you are recognized. An individual's turn generally can be as long as the number of points he has to make that are related to the topic under discussion. The black rule, on the other hand, is to come in when you can. This means waiting until a person has finished some point—it would be rude to attempt to claim the floor before at least one point has been made—and then come in. "Coming in" generally means engaging in argument on one or another point that has been raised or introducing an entirely new point. Should two or more people want to come in at the same time, precedence is usually negotiated by the principals themselves ("Let me just get this one point in"). Deference is often given to the person who feels his point is the most pressing ("I just have to say this!"). That person may acknowledge such courtesy by keeping this point concise so that the student who conceded a turn can take it fairly soon. Consideration may also be shown to a person of higher status due to age, experience, occupation, or general reputation. Because there is competition in claiming the floor, favored individuals are those who have a greater capacity for self-assertion than others or who can better manage to keep track of the pulse of the interaction and insert themselves in it a split second before someone else. Also helpful is sheer forcefulness in commanding the attention of others. Finally, because of the competitive nature of black turn-taking, occasionally two or more people are talking at the same time, though not necessarily to the same audience. Each speaker claims a group of listeners, so to speak, even if it is only a neighbor or those within the immediate vicinity. Listeners must decide whom to attend to. Sometimes several speakers are attended to at once. This pattern of listening to several speakers resembles closely the one Karl Reisman described among Afro-Antiguans (1974a, pp. 113–15).

If someone is trying to get into the debate but is having difficulty getting a turn and can get more assertive members to notice him, they will often intervene on his behalf. The person has to be seen as making an effort, however. Within one's own group, people who do not make an effort to join in are not usually asked why. It is assumed that those who feel they have something to say will be sufficiently moved by what they want to say to enter the debate. In a class with whites, in which the ratio is again 50:50, the same black attitude prevails initially until blacks become conscious that they are dominating the debate. It is at this point that the reticence or silence of whites itself becomes an issue.

Because the framework of argument governs black interaction, a turn rarely consists of more than two points if the issue is controversial. This is to allow others to answer the points that have been made if they so choose. Should someone use a turn to make a number of points, those who want to comment will object: "By the time you get through with all of your points, I will have forgotten your first point on which I wanted to make a comment." The issue here, however, is not only that those who wanted to get in will have forgotten their comments; the pattern and pulse of the interaction—the point and counterpoint of argument, as well as the spontaneous impulses to speak that the black pattern allows—will have been quelled by the impersonal manner of the presentation and the number of points made.

A good example of this occurred at a meeting, described by Joan McCarty, consisting mostly of black community people. The talk centered on male-female relationships. During the question-and-answer period, people were allowed to give their opinions. At one point, a man was giving his opinion when a woman said (after a point had been made, but before the man had finished all he wanted to say) "That's not true, that's not true . . . ." At this the black moderator—whom McCarty considered acculturated to middle-class norms—announced, "I just won't listen to any of you. You have to raise your hand. There's no debate, and you cannot ask a question of the person who made the statement." As a result, according to McCarty, "the heat level went down so low that it actually became boring to the people there, despite the fact that the issues were exciting."

Blacks and whites also differ in the conditions they set for taking a turn. For example, the white concept of turn-taking limits its authorization to the order of individual assertion. It would like, but does not require, a turn to be contingent upon the individual having something valuable to contribute. But a person can nonetheless be granted a turn without having anything important or even relevant to say, as when others show "democratic" concern that "everyone should have a turn." Black self-assertion within the framework of turn-taking is more strictly regulated with respect to content. Thus, if people insert themselves out of turn but nevertheless say something significant, their self-assertion will be considered "on time." Conversely, if someone's turn fits within the prescribed order but he says nothing worthwhile, others may challenge his self-assertion: "What did you come in with that for?" Within the black conception, the decision to enter the debate and assert oneself is self-determined, regulated entirely by individuals' own assessment of what they have to say. It is validated or not by the group afterward based only upon what was said. Within the white conception, an individual decision to enter the debate does not immediately translate into self-assertion. The impulse to assert oneself and speak must be checked. A turn has first to be requested and granted by an authorized person. Once the turn is granted, however, it needs no further authorization by audience validation of the content of what was said. The content might also be evaluated positively or negatively, but this has no bearing on the person's right to take a turn. The two are independently validated.

White turn-taking is authorized from without. Consequently it is seen as an entitlement, to be granted only to one person at a time, and to be terminated only by that person or the person empowered to grant turns. Whites are therefore chagrined to have their turn preempted before they are finished or infringed upon by other unauthorized conversations.

One reason that whites often find their turns preempted when interacting with blacks is that they do not cast their presentations within the framework of personal argument. Thus they may wish to make several successive points relevant to the topic. This blacks consider inappropriate since, according to the rules of argument, the truth value of each point has to be ascertained as closely as possible by those present before new points can be addressed. Moreover, all who want to are entitled to have their say before new points can be considered. Because blacks consider turns to consist of fewer points than do whites, they often come in to argue a point before whites have "finished." This whites consider rude. However, blacks believe a turn is over when a point has been made on which others wish to comment. Consequently they consider whites selfish for "hogging the floor" or not allowing the process of argument to be activated. It is then that blacks will attempt to take the floor, feeling that the white claim to undivided and noncompetitive attention has been forfeited. If they are unsuccessful in this, they may start another simultaneous conversation with whoever will participate in it.

Capacities

When the white student responded that she hardly ever spoke in class to the black request to hear from some of the white students in the room, she was attempting to convince the black students that her present classroom behavior was normal for her and, consequently, that her silence did not mean she was necessarily concealing something. The black students were reluctant to accept this for several reasons. I have already mentioned two: first, their disinclination to believe that she (and white students generally) would not have a position on a topic on which everyone could be expected to have a position (e.g., racism); second, the general black rule within argument—if you disagree with the view being expressed, you are obliged to speak up. This rule becomes internalized as an "impulse toward truth." If people disagree with a point, they will be sufficiently moved by that impulse to enter the debate. Silence therefore signifies agreement, but since it was unlikely that the white student agreed with everything that was said, they felt her silence had to have another explanation. But the black students' view was also influenced by what they assumed were the capacities of the white students to voice their disagreement if they had any. Blacks feel that the constraints against speaking up are caused by external factors that create risk: general regulations against speaking or the position of people in a minority. They do not see constraints against speaking as due to internal factors, i.e., psychological inhibitions. Consequently blacks feel that once external prohibitions against speaking have been lifted—that it is "safe" to speak—everyone should feel equally free to do so. This view implies that the capacities and inclinations of whites and blacks to assert themselves are equivalent. They are not.

The reason for this is that black culture allows its members considerably greater freedom to assert and express themselves than does white culture. Black culture values individually regulated self-assertion. It also values spontaneous expression of feeling. As a result, black cultural events typically encourage and even require individuals to behave in an assertive/expressive manner, as in such black speech events as *rapping* and *signifying* (Kochman 1970; Mitchell-Kernan 1971; Abrahams 1976), *call and response* (Daniel and Smitherman 1976), and, as I am claiming here, argument (Reisman 1974b).

White culture values the ability of individuals to rein in their impulses. White cultural events do not allow for individually initiated self-assertion or the spontaneous expression of feeling. Rather, self-assertion occurs as a social entitlement, a prerogative of one's higher status or, as with turn-taking, something granted and regulated by an empowered authority. And even when granted, it is a low-keyed assertion, showing detachment, modesty, understatement. Even play in white culture reflects the same norms. It is serious, methodical, and purposeful. "Showing off," which would represent individually initiated (unauthorized) self-assertion and more unrestrained self-expression, is viewed negatively within white culture. Black culture, on the other hand, views showing off—in black idiom *stylin' out, showboating, grandstanding*—positively (Holt 1972b).

Because white culture requires that individuals check those impulses that come from within, whites become able practitioners of self-restraint. However, this practice has an inhibiting effect on their ability to be spontaneously self-assertive. Consequently, white students find themselves at a disadvantage when engaging in debate with blacks. Not only is it easier for blacks to assert themselves—they can follow through on their impulses without having to wait for external authorization—but the level of energy and spiritual intensity that blacks generate is one that they can manage comfortably but whites can only manage with effort. As a result, whites find it difficult to establish the dynamic balance necessary to achieve parity for their opposing viewpoint.

Blacks do not initially see this relative mismatch, because they believe that their normal animated style is not disabling to whites. This belief is intensified on those occasions when white students of the counter-culture are present. Their style, like that of blacks, is animated, interpersonal, and argumentative. Their presence reinforces the black conviction that their own classroom mode is the standard way of engaging in public debate of an issue and makes them suspect even more those white students who claim that their quiet, unobtrusive behavior is their customary class-room style.

Self-Control

Whites are constrained not only by the higher level of energy and spiritual intensity that blacks generate. They are worried that blacks cannot sustain such intense levels of interaction without losing self-control. The reason for their concern is that whites conceive of and practice self-control as repression, checking impulses from within before they are released. Once such impulses are released, whites feel that self-control has been lost. Because they feel they are losing self-control when engaging in highly energetic and animated argument—the kind that functions for them as a ventilation of anger and hostility—they believe that no one else can successfully manage such intense exchanges. But blacks do not conceive of or practice self-control as repression. Rather—consistent with their cultural value upon assertive/expressive behavior—they see self-control as "getting it together": harmonizing the internal and external forces in the mode that black cultural events activate and release (Harrison 1972, p. xv). Internal forces are therefore controlled by the structure of the mode through which they are released. And, as Paul Carter Harrison said, "an emotion is never out of control when it fits the modality it is released in" (p. 157).

Other Disabling Factors

Two other factors interfere with the way blacks and whites initially relate to each other in the classroom. One is the rule among blacks, generally employed when they are in the minority or when the ratio of blacks to whites is about even, not to disagree with each other in front of whites. When this occurs, white students, who do not typically organize themselves in such a way, feel like isolated individuals pitted against a united black front. In conjunction with the more animated and energetic black style that whites find disabling, and their concern over blacks' ability to manage interaction at higher levels of spiritual intensity, this unified front further inhibits white participation. Of course this inhibition only increases black impatience with the white students' lack of participation (interpreted as intransigence), which leads to increased black pressure on whites to talk, which only intensifies white reluctance to speak, and so on. Not far into this process of escalation, whites begin to interpret black pressure as deliberate harrassment and think about dropping the class. A few white male students have indicated that they were ready to fight at this point, the intensity of the interaction having reached a level that they considered provocative.

It is usually at this time that I explain to the students what effect their behavior is having on each other. My description is often immediately confirmed by the students themselves. One white student remarked that he would ordinarily disagree more with things that had been said, since he is used to talking a lot in class, but here he felt "outnumbered." Frequently white students make such statements to me privately, but the risk this student took in speaking openly to the class raised his classroom stature among blacks, who appreciated the public admission of something honest and personal, and strengthened his own sense of personal security in class. It also effectively dissipated much of the impatience, frustration, and anger that blacks had begun to feel about general white lack of participation.

The other factor contributing to white silence is their fear that they will be chastised by blacks for personal views that they might reveal in response to requests to "hear from some of the white students in the room." Hence they are reluctant to comment on such a topic as racism when it is brought up—racism is usually the first subject on which blacks and whites interact seriously. The result is silence on the topic, and blacks then address whites individually regarding their personal viewpoint, with little success. What whites miss here is that blacks do not, as they think, want to elicit a personal admission of racism in order to condemn them. Rather, they want whites to acknowledge the extent to which racism has affected *everyone* in this country. Paradoxically, those who admit the effects of racism on themselves are perceived more positively by blacks than those who deny its effects. One white male student got considerable credit from black students when he said openly, "I know I'm a racist. I grew up in Belmont-

Craigin [an all-white working-class area in Chicago]. I'm working on it."

Changes

All that I have said here applies to blacks and whites interacting with each other during what I would call the initial phase of their coming together, lasting somewhere between one and two academic quarters. During the first quarter the full force of cultural ethnocentrism is at work. The meanings and values that each group attaches to the other's behavior are those of their own culture. How potent this ethnocentrism becomes in creating conflict also depends on how much forgiveness is present. Thus the disruptive potential of ethnocentric judgments is also a function of the general political climate of the times. The late 1960s and early 1970s were especially unforgiving, and some of the more contentious scenes described here occurred during this period. Even then, however, changes in behavior and attitudes became apparent after blacks and whites interacted with each other for a while. For example, white students began to revise their initial views that the more animated black mode was an attempt to intimidate them and dominate the proceedings. They did not reach the point of accepting the argumentative black mode as an equally valid means of getting at the truth, but they did come to see that blacks were not merely attempting to ventilate anger and hostility. Experiencing greater comfort, white students started to speak up more, thereby more nearly satisfying black expectations of greater verbal participation from white students.

In turn, black students began to concede that the dispassionate and detached white mode did not necessarily signify concealment or deviousness. On the other hand, they did not come to consider the impersonal presentation of ideas an acceptable alternative to argument as a means of testing the validity of an idea. Blacks also began to disagree with each other more, apparently no longer feeling the need to present themselves before whites as a united front on all issues.

In accidental or unmediated encounters, blacks and whites typically experience only the initial phase. Thus, in the meeting between community representatives and university faculty, members of the two groups held the same ethnocentric views of each other's behavior at the beginning and the end of the meeting. Each one accused the other of negotiating in bad faith, of introducing inappropriate behavioral elements into the process while simultaneously refusing admission of other elements that members of each group considered essential to the accomplishment of anything constructive.

Functionality and Dysfunctionality of Black and White Classroom Modalities

In practice, the ways that black and white debating processes are rendered dysfunctional is consistent with other areas of their respective cultural development. For example, in black cultural events generally, those with greater ability tend to dominate the proceedings as well as offer themselves as contenders against whom others can test their skills. Likewise, when engaging in debate, those who can assert themselves more successfully or who possess greater debating skills tend to dominate class interaction. While those who possess such skills generally can also be counted on to have more meaningful things to say, this is not always the case. Yet when it is not, I have observed that their dominance of the discussion is not always challenged, notwithstanding the black turn-taking rule that self-assertion is supposed to be regulated by an assessment of the content, which allows people to take the floor away from those who are not saying anything worthwhile. The reason such people are not always challenged is that blacks do not simply debate an idea; they debate the person debating the idea. Consequently, individuals in the group assess their own debating skills relative to others in the group, and if they feel they cannot generate the kind of dynamic balance necessary to establish parity for their view, they do not contend. The competitive aspect of claiming the floor and contending with the opposition within the black mode favors the more energetic, confident, assertive, and skillful individuals. The reluctance of less skillful individuals to contend defeats the ideal purpose of the group, to achieve the maximum truth value that all present are able to produce.

The white mode tends to debate the idea rather than the person debating the idea. This allows those who disagree to enter into the discussion without having to match the forcefulness of the opposition, since they are not in direct contention. This mode would seem to allow the greatest possible involvement, since participation is not dependent upon strong debating skills. And in practice, whites (and blacks) who do not enter a debate when it is governed by black norms participate when white norms prevail. Nonetheless, even within the less competitive and intense white framework, some individuals are still reluctant to assert themselves. And they cannot be made to do so if they choose not to. It is interesting to note that individuals' decision to assert themselves can be overruled by the empowered authority, but the decision *not* to assert themselves cannot be. Yet in some ways the latter disables the process of testing and validating ideas more severely than the former. For instance, it is easier for an instructor to suppress irresponsible self-assertion in a class than to overcome irresponsible nonassertion.

When pressed to account for their silence, whites use the rationalization that it is their right to do so, just as they have a right to their own opinion. Herbert Marcuse (1969) and Trevor Pateman (1975) have argued that the latter is a corruption of the free speech idea, and I consider their arguments to apply equally well to the "right" to remain silent.

Marcuse and Pateman base their arguments on the concept of free speech adopted by John Stuart Mill in *On Liberty:* namely, that free speech is to be governed by the impulse toward truth. People should be granted free speech so they will not be afraid to speak the truth. Freedom of speech was not intended to allow people to protect their views from being challenged under the rule that they have a *right* to their opinion, regardless of its irrational or inhumane content. "One could even claim that the fundamental right in classical liberal theory (as in Mill) is the right to dispossess people of their irrational ideas...not just to express an opinion, but to contribute to a debate...aiming at a positive outcome, in terms of the acceptance and application of one opinion rather than another" (Pateman 1975, p. 92). Similarly, a right to vote in a democracy becomes subverted by a claim for its converse: a right not to vote, which American citizens also hold, despite its debilitating effect on basic democratic processes. The right to remain silent is the same corruption of the free speech concept as the "right to one's own opinion." The goal for which freedom of speech was obtained—the pursuit of truth—becomes subverted by the right to remain silent. In Marcuse's terms, tolerance that was promoted as a means to an end, in becoming an end unto itself has become repressive of the goal it was originally intended to promote (Marcuse 1969, p. 82). When individuals insist upon their right to remain silent during a debate, they also withhold the presentation of another idea and thus work against the realization of a better collective truth. By way of contrast, the black view that one is obliged to contribute to a debate, especially if one disagrees, is consistent with the Millian ideal in satisfying the impulse toward truth that was the goal for which tolerance of free speech was originally obtained.

The white cultural idea that individuals should approach an issue with an open mind is based on the conception that one side in a disagreement is not likely to have a monopoly on the truth. But the idea of "keeping an open mind," like the idea of free speech, was conceived as a means of arriving at a better truth. It was intended as a mode of inquiry, a stance to be taken when people do not yet feel they have sufficient information to form an opinion, and here it functions to advantage. It becomes dysfunctional when it becomes an end in itself, a state of indefinite mental suspension, to be maintained without regard to the relative merits of the different views being advanced. Yet this is often what occurs.

That it does so is not surprising. It is the logical consequence of a process of schooling that typically asks students simply to research and report information on issues, to present the views of both sides, not to develop a personal position with respect to either one. Thus prospective school teachers take a required philosophy of education course which basically asks them to read and feed back the ideas of John Dewey and others. But they are not also asked to consider, let alone debate, which of these views are more persuasive to them and why. Their own ideas do not count. Credit is given only for knowing "authoritative" ideas.

This process is dysfunctional in satisfying the impulse toward truth in that it does not encourage the activation of independent thought processes. Consequently a group does not benefit from

the different intellectual capacities of its membership except insofar as one or another is better able to grasp and articulate the
authorized viewpoint. This defeats the ideal process of inquiry
and challenge that presumes that the collection of individuals
engaged in debate will be sufficiently independent-minded so that
qualitatively different views will be debated and will produce a
better truth. Everyone engaged in producing only authorized
viewpoints will produce authorized viewpoints. Similarly, if students are not given the opportunity to test their own ideas, they
do not develop these ideas, because they are not confronted with
situations that require independent ideas. Nor do they see creating a personal position as the logical end result of an exhaustive
inquiry into different sides of an issue.

The black notion of accepting personal responsibility for the
views that one presents requires individuals to develop a personal
position. This posture contrasts with the posture of whites when
engaging in debate in ways that I have already mentioned. But it
also affects the way black and white students respond to questions asked by an instructor. As Allen Harris, one of my students,
observed, "I've noticed that when an instructor asks a question
of white students, they tend to give him back what he has just said
on the subject. Black students, on the other hand, tend to give
their own opinion."

In the course of a lifetime of experience in expressing personal
positions, blacks are compelled in debate to activate their own
thinking about any idea that is presented and that has not already
been tested by them and found to be true. In the most important
of such debates, blacks and whites cannot be said to be debating
an issue; rather, they are negotiating an issue.

Negotiating

Discussion and argument in a college classroom differ from such
activities in formal negotiating sessions. There are at least three
important differences between classroom encounters and meetings like those between Trotter and Wilson, between representatives of the black community and college faculties, and public
meetings between blacks and whites in general.

First, the goal of negotiations in formal situations is not to determine who can establish the greater claim to fact, reason, logic, or humaneness but, rather, to effect a course of action. Thus negotiating is not simply debate: arguments are means to an end, not an end in themselves. Second, the nature of the inequality of the participants is different. In the classroom, inequality results from the greater ability of one student, or one group of students, to argue well. In official meetings, inequality is built into the negotiations. It results from the power of one group—in situations like those I have described, the whites—to prevail regardless of the merits of their argument. Third, grievances are involved, not just issues; since blacks are a minority group in American society, they are generally the aggrieved party. Consequently, the stance blacks take in the classroom is intensified in official meetings. What is expressed is not only earnestness and dynamic opposition but also anger and hostility.

Whites react to this anger and hostility in negotiating sessions in much the same way that white students react to emotional expression in the classroom: they consider it disabling to what they regard as a rational process. Consequently they feel that passion, prejudice, fear, and hatred should be set aside before negotiations even begin (Wicker 1975, p. 45).

Blacks do not believe that emotions interfere with their capacity to reason. Trotter's argument to Wilson was no less cogent, for example, because it was emotional. Blacks certainly cannot agree that the expression of anger and hostility by an aggrieved party is inappropriate during negotiating sessions. After all, they are reacting to the conditions and circumstances that constitute the agenda of the meeting. Blacks regard white efforts to get them to set aside their feelings as unrealistic, illogical, and politically devious. It is unrealistic to demand that an emotion be separated from its cause. It is illogical to ask aggrieved parties to do so before any concessions are made to them. It is politically devious as an attempt by whites to gain, as a prerequisite to negotiations, what they want as a consequence of the negotiations, i.e., appeasement of black anger and hostility. If whites were able to attain this result before negotiating, they would, in effect, attain it without negotiating at all. For all these reasons, blacks are sensitive and alert to attempts to discredit their anger and hostility as inappropriate or unwarranted. Were they to agree to set aside their anger before the circumstances that created it were corrected, they would be conceding that the grievances could not have been that serious.

Blacks also feel that whites are hypocritical when they ask that everyone "please stay calm so we can continue with the meeting," because they know that such calm is easier for whites, who are not the aggrieved party, to achieve. When whites leave a meeting room because blacks cannot "stay calm," blacks regard their departure cynically, as an admission that they were not ready to negotiate, rather than the strong statement about rules of conduct that whites claim to be making.

Tom Wicker's account of the 1971 prison rebellion at Attica reflects the differences in black and white points of view on negotiation. Observers were present to promote negotiation between the prisoners and the state officials. The middle-class observers, white, black, and Puerto Rican, reflected the white view, and began with the premise that the anger and defiance of the prisoners had to be dealt with *before* negotiation could properly begin. Thus, Alfredo Mathew, a Puerto Rican school superintendent from New York City, scolded another observer, Jaybarr Kenyatta, a black community leader from Harlem, a Muslim and a former inmate at Attica himself, for inflaming the situation with his rhetoric rather than calming things down. "How could Kenyatta expect, if he urged the inmates on, that they would achieve a conciliatory mood?" (Wicker 1975, p. 118).

Another observer, after many hours of listening to the prisoners' defiant speeches, asked when the inmates would be ready to negotiate. This reflected the failure of most observers to recognize that the defiant speeches of the inmates fell within the framework of negotiations—actually *were* the negotiations and were "so regarded by the inmates and the state" (Wicker, p. 116). The observers were there in response to the prisoners' demand that their grievances become part of the public record; the very appearance of the observers was a concession that the inmates had wrung from the state.

Although the situation at Attica was much more dramatic than most negotiating sessions, it occurred, like most negotiating sessions, precisely because of the anger of the aggrieved party. The prisoners had rebelled, had taken hostages, and had resolved to kill them. It was their anger, determination, and defiance that had brought the observers and outside officials to the prison. Without this emotional underpinning, the prisoners might not have been able to sustain the intensity necessary to make their threat real: thus, in their view, they would have lost their power to force the negotiations to continue rather than, as the white observers believed, strengthened their bargaining position.

Negotiations between officials and minority groups often break down. Because the stakes were very high at Attica, the breakdown of negotiations resulted in bloodshed and death. Nelson Rockefeller, governor of New York, grew impatient at the loss of official control of the prison and ordered his state troopers to move in. The result was an immediate loss of lives among both prisoners and guards. Less intense negotiations between blacks and whites also break down, and we have to wonder why.

In general, whites take a view of the negotiating procedure that is markedly different from the view taken by blacks. Though blacks regard whites as devious in insisting that emotions be left in front of the meeting-room door, whites think that blacks are being devious by insisting on bringing those emotions into the room. If the meeting is to be successful, the blacks' anger and hostility will be allayed by the results of the meeting. Therefore, for blacks to insist on behaving emotionally is to prejudge the outcome of negotiations. Blacks simply do not see things this way. To leave their emotions aside is not their responsibility; it is the whites' responsibility to provide them first with a reason to do so.

The requirement to behave calmly, rationally, unemotionally, and logically when negotiating is looked upon by blacks as a political requirement—and to accede to it in advance is considered as a political defeat. They believe that whites should take the first step to make meetings less emotional by proposing an agenda that includes concessions to the black position. This is especially true because they are meeting with agents of the group they hold responsible for creating their grievances in the first place. On the other hand, it may not even occur to whites that their requirements for calm and unemotional negotiation have political implications.

Whites may not feel that they are asking people to be more conciliatory when they ask them to allay their anger sufficiently to negotiate an issue. An impersonal, uninvolved discussion is the kind of discussion to which whites in official positions are accustomed. When negotiating, diplomats do not have to endorse or become emotionally involved in one outcome or another. As we have seen, however, discussion is not argument. In discussion, one can be dispassionate; in argument, when one's own needs and views matter, it is much more difficult, and sometimes injurious to one's cause, to sound dispassionate. Moreover, it is possible that the ability to remain dispassionate can be achieved only by those who have worked long and hard to separate thought from feeling.

It is also possible that those who have succeeded in separating thought from feeling are able to do so only when they have nothing at stake. There are times, of course, when everyone has something at stake. Financially secure whites say, ''I worked for what I have. I wanted it.'' Blacks may say, ''I fought for it'' or ''I struggled for it.'' All important accomplishments of individuals have an emotional background—wanting, needing. When something is at stake, any reduction in the emotional need for it can be considered disabling. However effective may be the reduction of emotion in moving a discussion along, it is disabling to the one who *needs* the outcome to be favorable or the one who wants it enough. Stripping the outcome of its emotional component may very well have the effect, certainly in official negotiations, of making one's opponent less rigid, more flexible, less insistent on winning every point—and therefore easier to deal with. Nonetheless, as long as anger remains a vital force in a room, it must be dealt with.

The solution to political conflicts between blacks and whites, if there is one, may not lie within the rules of negotiating that the white establishment has created for the powerless. Negotiating sessions are often conducted in official buildings that look like Roman temples, which disconcert black negotiators even as they enter. In such structures, the venting of emotion is far less acceptable than it might be in a neighborhood storefront or in a black church. Yet the very architecture of the official building makes it more important to black negotiators to sustain the emotion that brought them there. Moreover, the marble inside represents the power of the establishment and thus serves to reinforce the grievance and heighten the emotion.

The most obvious way of avoiding the anger or hostility in a prison or a hearing room is to pay attention to it earlier, before it has come to a head. It takes more than one broken promise before people come to disbelieve each other. Mutual suspicion between blacks and whites has become much more common in our society than mutual trust, and it is within this kind of atmosphere that most negotiations take place. Understanding the other's point of view and way of arguing is important, but it may be even more important for whites to understand that the conflict is often a political one and that there are real issues to be resolved—issues far more important than the manners of either party.

Three

Fighting Words

Scene 1

At the meeting between community representatives and university faculty referred to in chapter 2, the remark of the white female faculty member who characterized the session as a "Baptist revival meeting" did not go unchallenged. A black male faculty member—a principal leader in the opposition to the proposed urban education program—angrily pointed a finger at her and said, "Professor ———, you need to know something. You can't make me over into your image. Do you understand that? You can't make me over into your image." Then, upon seeing her frightened look, he softened his anger and said, "You don't need to worry; I'm still talking. When I *stop* talking, then you might need to worry." The white professor was not reassured. When the meeting was over, she accused the black faculty member of having "threatened" her. He was astonished by her accusation. His comment to me afterward was, "All I did was *talk* to her. Now how can that be threatening?"

These conflicting interpretations of the black professor's behavior are not unique to this encounter. Whites *invariably* interpret black anger and verbal aggressiveness as more provocative and threatening than do blacks. Two further examples will illustrate this claim.

Scene 2

In a CBS television program entitled "Justice in America: Some Are More Equal Than Others," broadcast on April 20, 1971, eleven jurors who had served during the trial of a member of the Black Panther party discussed the thinking they had gone through to reach a verdict. The defendant had been charged with illegal possession of firearms and with conspiracy. The legal determination of the first charge was clear-cut: the jury needed only to find that the accused had firearms in his automobile when he was stopped by the police. And so they did find.

The charge of conspiracy, however, was more complicated. It originated in the state's contention that Panther party statements like "Off the pig," contained in literature also found in the accused's car, should be interpreted literally: as constituting a declaration of intent of individual party members as well as a directive to other blacks to kill policemen.

During the telecast, one of the white jurors said that he and the other white jurors had initially agreed with the prosecution's interpretation of such published statements as *threats*. All of the seven black jurors, however, had interpreted them as *rhetoric*. As a consequence of the exchange of the two interpretations, the charge of conspiracy was not sustained.

Scene 3

In Louisville, Kentucky, a white female teacher had begun to teach black high school students for the first time. She drew this assignment as a result of the city's desegregation of its schools. In the classroom, two black male students began a loud dispute over which of them had the right to a particular seat. Each assumed a menacing confrontational stance toward the other. No punches were actually thrown. Nevertheless, the teacher sent the two students to the principal's office for fighting.

At the end of the class period, several black students came up to her to question her decision. They said, "Why did you send them to the principal's office for fighting? They weren't going to do anything!" Yet the teacher felt certain that blows were about to be exchanged. Moreover, in her report of the incident, she said that she felt the "fight" had already begun when the two youths started to get loud and angry.

The consistently different interpretations that blacks and whites give to this type of black aggressive behavior arises from the specific meaning of such behavior within each cultural group. In this chapter I will identify the significant differences in the conventions of aggressive behavior within the two cultures that give rise to these interpretations. I will also demonstrate the effect of other cultural assumptions that have been identified in chapter 2.

Aggressive Behavior in the Black and White Communities
Conceptual Frameworks

When does a fight begin? One important factor in the ways blacks and whites interpret black aggressive behavior is their conception of when a fight begins. Whites consider "fighting" to have begun when violence is imminent, that is, before violence has actually occurred. Typically, the fight is considered to have started upon a loud public dispute and the establishment of confrontation, as in the case of the teacher in Scene 3. But there are also other signs that indicate to whites that a fight has begun: the intensity of the anger that is shown and the presence of insults. Together they create among whites the feeling that violence is imminent. Should threats also occur, these reinforce for whites what the other behavior already indicates; it establishes that the violence about to occur is intentional and not simply the result of a dispute "getting out of hand."

Significantly, while blacks consider all of these signs relevant in setting the stage for fighting to occur, they do not consider them sufficient to conclude that a fight has actually begun. This is because for blacks the boundary between words and actions is clearly marked. Consequently they would say the parties involved were "having an argument" or, if there were threats and insults and challenges to fight, they might be *woofing*. But arguing or woofing is still not "fighting." Conceptually blacks still consider it within the framework of talking. Fighting does not begin until someone actually makes a provocative *movement*. As Allen Harris put it,

> if two guys are talking loud and then one or the other starts to reduce the distance between them, that's a sign, because it's important to get in the first blow. Or if a guy puts his hand in his pocket, and that's not a movement he usually makes, then you watch for that—he might be reaching for a knife. But if they're just talking—doesn't matter how loud it gets—then you got nothing to worry about.

A good illustration of how warily blacks attend to movement during a dispute is contained in a recording entitled "The Flying Saucer Song." Two black men are in a bar, and A is trying to convince B that the strange light he saw the other evening was a flying saucer. B refuses to take A seriously:

> *B:* Shit! You know something? You're crazy. You know that?
> *A:* Hey. Don't you call me crazy, man.... What would you have done, man?
> *B:* Well, to begin with I wouldn't have told this story. You understand?
> *A:* That's easy for you to say. But it happened to me....
> *B:* Listen, man. Don't be some asshole. You tryin' to pull my—
> *A:* Hey! You called me an asshole....
> *B:* It's just that you *are* an asshole, understand?
> *A:* Hey, you know something? You know what's going to happen to you?
> *B:* Now, listen. Don't you raise that glass, understand?
> *A:* Hey! You know what I could do if I wanted to get.... Hey, you going to make me angry here. I'm just trying to talk to you.... [Nilsson 1975]

Were B a white man, he would probably have felt violence was imminent when A said, "You know what's going to happen to you?" He might even have felt the "fight" had started when B said, "It's just that you *are* an asshole, understand?" But being a black man, B attended to movement, not loud, abusive talk. Thus he said, "Don't you raise that glass, understand?" A's response was to clarify: "I'm just trying to *talk* to you." If he had picked up the glass at that critical moment, B would have considered it a provocative move, one that signaled a fight. Similarly, when we were discussing this point, Lillie Kitchen, one of my black students, remembered that a fight she had had in high school "started" when the other girl reached into her purse during an argument.

A large television audience saw the effect of a provocative move during a confrontation between Muhammad Ali and Joe Frazier, when they were interviewed by Howard Cosell on ABC's *Wide World of Sports* after their first fight. As usual, when these two got together in public, they began to woof at (insult) each other. Typically Ali, being the more verbally adept, scored most of the points. This time, after he called Frazier "ignant" (from "ignorant," but meaning "grossly stupid"), Frazier rose from his chair and stood directly in front of Ali, who was still sitting down.

At that point, both men's handlers appeared on the screen. Rather than wait to see what Frazier was going to do, Ali grabbed his arms and held them down until the handlers could separate them. Later Ali admitted that he did not know what Frazier was going to do. Nonetheless, Frazier's move was a real provocation, and neither Ali nor the others present were going to wait to see how he would follow it up.

In this case, the provocation was clear, but a continuation of the fight was averted. However, during the 1977–78 National Basketball Association season, actual violence between Kermit Washington, a black player, and Rudy Tomjanovich, a white one, was not. According to Tomjanovich, he tried to break up a fight that he thought was about to erupt between Washington and someone else. Washington, however, interpreted Tomjanovich's movement toward him as provocative, signaling an intent to hit him. Following the rule that it is important to get in the first blow Washington swung first and broke Tomjanovich's jaw.

The black jurors who interpreted the Black Panthers' statements as rhetoric rather than threats (Scene 2) took into account the fact that the Panthers had made no actual move to kill police officers. Until they did, they were still only "talking." The black students in Scene 3 who concluded that their classmates were not going to do anything probably noticed a similar absence of aggressive movement.

Patterns of Behavior

It was not only the absence of any provocative move by the Black Panthers or the two students in the Louisville classroom that influenced the black interpretation of their verbally aggressive behavior. Knowledge of the cultural conventions surrounding such behavior was also involved. These conventions hold that angry verbal disputes, even those involving insults and threats, can be maintained by blacks at the verbal level *without* violence necessarily resulting. As R. Lincoln Keiser reported from his fieldwork among the Vice Lords of Chicago, "There are two kinds of behavior that are expected in situations of enmity. Vice Lords call these 'woofing' and 'humbugging.' Woofing is the exchange of insults and challenges to fight, while humbugging is actual fighting.... Rivals can play out their social interaction solely in terms of woofing" (1969, p. 44).

White conventions of aggressive behavior do not generate a similar conceptual boundary between words and actions. Rather, whites tend to see the public expression of hostility as a point on a words–actions continuum: angry verbal exchanges, if not stopped, will inevitably escalate into violence. Within this conception, hostile words and hostile acts become different forms of the same thing—fighting. White couples will say that they had a "fight" when all they had was an argument. But when you hear a black husband and wife say they had a "fight," as Allen Harris put it, "physical blows were struck; they weren't just arguing." An example of this usage can be found in the statement of one black woman who said, "When I was married to my first husband we fought all the time. Once he knocked me around so bad I ended up in the hospital for three days" (in Day 1974, p. 200).

The notion of hostile words leading inevitably to violence affected all of the interpretations given by whites in the examples above. The white faculty member in Scene 1 was afraid that the anger of her black counterpart might escalate into violence. This assumption undoubtedly also influenced the conclusion of the white teacher in Scene 3 that a "fight" had already begun. The white jurors in Scene 2 were also operating under this assumption, but more specifically, as applied to threats.

Threats and Woofing

Threats in the white community are always interpreted as true indicators of intent to act, and on a short timetable. Consequently they are always provocative. This accounts for the white cultural rule "Don't make threats unless and until you are prepared to carry them out." It also explains why the white jurors in Scene 2 interpreted the statements of the Black Panthers as threats. They had no cultural reference for a pattern of behavior in which threats would be made but not acted upon. Blacks do have this pattern of behavior in woofing. On the streets its purpose is to gain, without actually having to become violent, the respect and fear from others that is often won through physical combat. To accomplish this it is necessary to create an image of being fearless and tough, someone not to be trifled with. Once someone's reputation in these respects has been established, he may never again be called upon to prove it and can then walk the streets with impunity. Elliot Liebow describes Tally, one of his principal street-corner respondents, in just such terms.

> He is six feet tall and weighs just under two hundred pounds. His size and carriage lend credibility to the general belief that he was once a professional heavyweight fighter. When asked to affirm or deny this status, Tally merely grins, assumes the classic stance of the boxer, and invites the questioner to "come on." No one does. [Liebow 1966, p. 23]

Blacks generally recognized the posture of the Black Panthers as woofing. One black man from Mobile called it that while disparaging it as a tactic: "All that wolfing [woofing], and now y'all got gun control worse than ever" (in Murray 1971, p. 278).

But simply to recognize the activity as woofing is not to say that blacks can necessarily tell whether those woofing will actually do what they propose. This is because the facade is often the same whether the person is serious or not. Moreover, to produce the desired effect generally requires that those woofing create an aura of drama surrounding themselves to keep people wondering if they are in fact serious. Muhammad Ali provided some examples of this at the weigh-in ceremony before his first fight with Sonny Liston and in the confrontation with Joe Frazier outside Frazier's gym in Philadelphia. In his book Ali tells us that both encounters were staged. Nonetheless, he notes that Frazier still had difficulty at one point determining whether he was being serious or not. "His eyes are blazing and I know suddenly that the pretense is gone and this is no put-on. Joe has always been a little slow in making out whether or not I'm serious or putting on" (Ali 1975, p. 259). But Ali was such a good actor that even those people close to him often could not tell when he was being serious. Thus once, when Ali was really hurt from a punch during training, he slid slowly down the ropes to the canvas. On the way down, Ali reported,

> I see some startled faces, wide eyes, the crowd in the gym rushing up to the ring: "Is he hurt?" ... "Is he faking?" ... I stretch out on the canvas and feel Bundini's arms lifting my shoulders, his mouth to my ear. "You sure make it look real, Champ." ... He's seen me go through this act a dozen times just to liven up the gym—but now he's not sure what it is. [1975, p. 292]

The difficulty for blacks in detecting whether woofing is serious lies not only in the ability of the persons woofing to conceal their true feelings. It is complicated by the almost indistinguishable line between being serious and mock serious: showing *and* feeling anger and fearlessness versus simply showing them. Ali was able to detect when Frazier was no longer putting on ("His eyes are blazing and I know suddenly that the pretense is gone and this is no put-on"), but he also observed that Frazier had difficulty detecting Ali's own attitude. There are other documented examples of this confusion. James Maryland describes a woofing exchange between Sweet Red and Black Power—Maryland used the term *signifying*—which had grown in intensity. As a result, "the crowd made fewer and fewer comments, not sure of whether or not the two participants were still signifying or were 'for real'" (1972, pp. 212–13).

Perhaps it is because of this difficulty that blacks have shifted their attention from aggressive posturing to movement, considering the latter a more reliable indicator of imminent violence. Paradoxically, woofing is now often a sign that those involved do *not* intend to use physical force, that they are relying on the drama created by woofing to accomplish the same end. This seems to have been implied in the black faculty member's statement in Scene 1: "You don't need to worry; I'm still talking. When I *stop* talking, then you might need to worry." Another implication of his statement is that angry disputes *can* be sustained at the verbal level without necessarily becoming violent. This implication is also contained in his other statement: "All I did was *talk* to her. Now how can that be threatening?"

Given this convention of aggressive speech behavior in the black community—that woofing is still just "talking"—the black jurors in Scene 2 had no other option than to interpret the statements of the Black Panthers as rhetoric.

Capacities

The different black and white perspectives on whether angry disputes can be contained at the verbal level derive from their different degrees of confidence in their ability to manage hostile and intense confrontations without losing self-control.

White confidence in this area is quite low, because whites practice self-control as repression. Consequently they become skilled only in reining in impulses and have little practice in managing these forces once they have been released. When whites become angry and express their anger, therefore, they have lost self-control; and others around them take this as a sign to move in to control the situation for them. Thus, third parties will exhort the antagonists to keep calm, tell one or both to quiet down, and should it be necessary, try to reduce the intensity of their opposition by keeping them apart physically.

The confidence of blacks in their ability to manage anger and hostility at the verbal level without losing self-control is higher. This is due to the greater freedom of assertion and expression allowed in black culture that also develops their ability to manage higher levels of heat and affect without becoming overwhelmed. This does not imply that no outer limits exist for blacks; rather, the level of intensity reached before the question of self-control arises will be higher for blacks than for whites. A situation that may seem to whites impossible to manage can seem quite manageable to blacks. An illustration of this difference can be found in the behavior of black and white basketball coaches in the NBA. As Jeff Greenfield observed, black coaches exhibit far less emotion on the bench than their white counterparts: "K. C. Jones and Bill Russell are statuelike compared with Tommy Heinsohn, Jack Ramsey, or Dick Motta" (1975, p. 170). White coaches find themselves less able to manage the high levels of heat and affect that the tension of close games invariably produces.

The question of self-control may be applied both to loud disputations and to verbal abuse. What occurs in black culture, beyond the more general development of assertive and expressive behavior, that would enhance the ability of blacks to manage specifically the much greater verbal intensity of woofing without loss of self-control? Part of the answer at least must lie in the experience of blacks in growing up, engaging in games of verbal insult like *sounding* and *playing the dozens*. Also relevant is the more general relationship that exists between the world of play and the real world.

The Role of Verbal Play

Gregory Bateson (1972, pp. 14–20), Erving Goffman (1974, pp. 40–82), and Roger Abrahams (1976, pp. 40–41), among others, have pointed out that the concept of *play* implies an ability to differentiate play from the "real" and the "serious." Furthermore, for play to function effectively as play, "there must be a sense of threat arising from the 'real' and 'serious' world of behavior" (Abrahams 1976, p. 40). But to create this sense of threat, play must approach the border of the real, must give the impression, through almost exact simulation, that what is going on is "for real," even though it is not. This is what occurs in woofing. Especially when it is not clear that it is an act, as in the staged confrontation between Ali and Frazier, it generates the same tension and drama as aggression that is "for real." But there is always danger as the boundaries between playful and real aggression begin to blur. Playful aggression retains a potential for becoming serious, and the closer it comes to resembling serious aggression, the greater its potential for actually becoming serious. This is well illustrated in Maryland's account of the confrontation between Sweet Red, a pimp, and Black Power, a former pimp turned preacher, at a shoe-shine stand. Red is trying to ease out of the confrontation without losing face, but Pretty Black, a third party, won't let him. When Red makes a move to the door, saying, "I'm going to step now, and make this little run," Pretty Black stops him with "Running to what, and from Black Power?" Red responds with annoyance: "Man, motherfuck you and Black Ass Power." This retort moves the verbal exchange further along the path toward seriousness, raising the level of tension of both the participants and the crowd, which at this point "whooped and hollered with laughter, for they knew the signifying was really on." The following exchange increases the tension still further:

Black Power: "Pity a poor fool brothers, for he knoweth not what's happening. He's a lost sheep in a pasture of white bullshit."

Sweet Red (shouting angrily): "Lost my ass, nigger! What about all that shit that you've been pulling with them damn white hippie bitches? You going around here with that damn white collar turned backwards talking shit about you being somebody's savior from the East! You ain't shit! Some of these young *real* black brothers ought to beat that holy shit outa you!"

At this point the crowd begins to make "fewer and fewer comments, not sure of whether or not the two participants were still signifying or were 'for real.'" Playful and serious verbal aggression have become indistinguishable. Black Power keeps the tension at this level when he says, pointing to three bearded black men wearing dashikis who are walking toward the stand, "What I ought to do is call them young brothers over here to investigate these white whore-hungry niggers." At this point Red becomes uneasy. There exists the danger that the domain of serious aggression will be penetrated. Others sense this also and therefore try to return the confrontation to a less volatile level. Pretty Black directs the play toward Cotton, a wino, saying, "Damn Cotton, wake up and turn your head the other way, cause your funky breath smells like rat piss." Black Power also tries to ease the tension by saying, "Don't be scared son, I come to save you and not to condemn you nigger. I've been commissioned to help niggers like you." Red responds, "The only help you can give me is to buy my smokes and rent my ladies." The tension has eased, but only a bit. It needs to be reduced still further. Pretty Black says to Red, grinning, "Now that ain't hip, Blood, telling a preacher that kind of shit." At this Black Power jumps back in, saying "Don't worry baby, before this devil-lover leaves here, that lye in his hair is either gonna eat the sickness outta this nigger's head or eat up his damn brains." At this remark, the anger and tension diminishes. The borderline between playful and real aggression once again becomes clear. Red says, "Say, Rev., tell them 'bout the little white lady that called you all of the Black M.F.'s and S.O.B.'s at Big Joe's party last Christmas." As Maryland says, Red is now assured "that he and Black Power were only signifying and working a game on each other with their raps" (Maryland 1972, pp. 212–13).

In contests like these, where the tension is raised and the threat from the real world is greatest, blacks develop and test their ability to take verbal abuse without resorting to violence. As H. Rap Brown remarks, "We exercised our minds by playing the dozens" (1969, p. 27). This self-discipline serves blacks well later, in situations where verbal aggression is or can become a serious matter. Thus, even though the staged verbal confrontation between Muhammad Ali and Joe Frazier suddenly became serious for Frazier, both men were still able to withstand each other's verbal assaults and maintain the public expression of their antagonism at the verbal level.

Whites do not engage in verbal insult as an extended activity. In my group, growing up in New York City, insults consisted of one-line openers and retorts like the following:

A: Got a match?
B: Yeah, my ass and your face.

or

    My farts and your breath.

William Labov found similar patterns in New York City:

A: Eat shit.
B: What should I do with the [your] bones?
A: Build a cage for your mother.
B: At least I got one.
A: She *is* the least. [Labov 1972b, p. 321]

This kind of verbal play did not generate much heat or tension. It certainly did not serve to develop the kind of self-discipline necessary to withstand verbal abuse without becoming violent. It hardly compares with the level of intensity or verbal activity that blacks reach in sounding or playing the dozens, as the following example, collected by James Maryland, shows.

Frank looked up and saw Leroy enter the Outpost. Leroy walked past the room where Quinton, Nap, Pretty Black, Cunny, Richard, Haywood, Bull, and Reese sat playing cards. As Leroy neared the T.V. room, Frank shouted to him.

Frank: "Hey, Leroy, your mama—calling you man."

Leroy turned and walked toward the room where the sound came from. He stood in the door and looked at Frank.

Leroy: "Look motherfuckers, I don't play that shit."
Frank (signifying): "Man, I told you cats 'bout that mama jive" *(as if he were concerned about how Leroy felt).*
Leroy: "That's all right Frank; you don't have to tell those funky motherfuckers nothing; I'll fuck me up somebody yet."

Frank's face lit up as if he were ready to burst his side laughing. Cunny became pissed at Leroy.

Cunny: "Leroy, you stupid bastard, you let Frank make a fool of you. *He* said that 'bout your mama."
Pretty Black: "Aw, fat ass head, Cunny shut up."
Cunny: "Ain't that some shit. This black slick head motor flicker got nerve 'nough to call somebody fathead. Boy, you so black, you sweat super Permalube Oil."

This eased the tension of the group as they burst into loud laughter.

Pretty Black: "What'chu laughing 'bout Nap, with your funky mouth smelling like dog shit."

Even Leroy laughed at this.

Nap: "Your mama motherfucker."
Pretty Black: "Your funky mama too."
Nap (strongly): "It takes twelve barrels of water to make a steamboat run; it takes an elephant's dick to make your Grandmammy come; she been elephant fucked, camel fucked and hit side the head with your Grandpappy's nuts."
Reese: "Goddor damn; go on and rap motherfucker."

Reese began slapping each boy in his hand, giving his approval of Nap's comment. Pretty Black, in an effort not to be outdone but directing his verbal play elsewhere, stated:

Pretty Black: "Reese, what you laughing 'bout? You so square you shit bricked shit."

Frank: "Whoooowee!"

Reese (sounded back): "Square huh, what about your nappy ass hair before it was stewed; that shit was so bad till, when you went to bed at night, it would leave your head and go on the corner and meddle."

The boys slapped each other in the hand and cracked up.

Pretty Black: "On the streets meddling, bet Dinky didn't offer me no pussy and I turned it down."

Frank: "Reese scared of pussy."

Pretty Black: "Hell yeah; the greasy mother rather fuck old, ugly, funky cock Sue Willie than get a piece of ass from a decent broad."

Frank: "Goddor damn! Not Sue Willie."

Pretty Black: "Yeah, ol' meat beating Reese rather screw that cross-eyed, clapsy bitch, who when she cry, tears drip down her ass."

Haywood: "Don't be so mean, Black."

Reese: "Aw shut up, you half-white bastard."

Frank: "Wait man, Haywood ain't gonna hear much more of that half-white shit; he's a brother too."

Reese: "Brother, my black ass; that white ass landlord gotta be this motherfucker's paw."

Cunny: "Man, you better stop foolin' with Haywood; he's turning red."

Haywood: "Fuck yall" *(as he withdrew from the "sig" game).*

Frank: "Yeah, fuck yall; let's go to the stick hall."

[In Kochman 1970, pp. 158–59]

Such verbal insult as sounding is not always containable at the verbal level. This is especially true when it occurs outside the boundaries of one's own group, whose moderating influence is often necessary to keep the level of aggression from becoming serious, as the examples above have shown. Thus, when Haywood was being sounded on by one of his best friends in the presence of two ladies, while other members of the group were absent, he refused to tolerate it. He went home, came back with a rifle, and shot and killed his friend. Similarly, Daniel Swett reported that the shooting of Chicago Eddie by Young Beartracks outside a pool room in Palo Alto was provoked in part by Chicago Eddie putting Young Beartracks "in the dozens" (Swett 1969, p. 98). Nonetheless, the fact that such verbal insult as sounding can also function as play often allows the target of the abuse to treat the insult as play rather than as a real provocation, even if it was intended as provocation. Tom Wicker describes an example of this. It occurred in 1946, on a troop train that was to take him and other sailors from Seattle to Virginia to be discharged. The trip would take about two weeks. Wicker was put in charge of a car that contained two other whites and twenty-seven blacks. Soon after the train started, a tall black sailor called out, "Hey you, Red!" According to Wicker, "silence fell on the car like soot from a steam engine." After Wicker replied, "Yeah," the black sailor said, "Suck my black dick." Wicker said half the blacks laughed, a little uncertainly, and one or two eyed him stonily. He could not tell whether he was being teased or challenged. Nonetheless, he was "astonished . . . that the tall black thought there was any reason to be hostile, even more astonished that a black man would dare to speak so to a white." He had to respond, but how? He could deal with this black youth as a "Southern white man would deal with a colored person, whether nigger, nigruh, or Negro, and back it up; or else he would have to deal with him as one human with another and live with the consequences." Wicker decided on the latter course of action. An old joke flickered in his memory. "Why, your buddy there told me you didn't even have one. Said a hog bit it off." The black sailor grinned, and the other blacks laughed. He replied, "Shee-it. You git home, man, you ask your girl friend, see if I ain't broke it off in her pussy." Wicker responded, "After mine, I reckon she wouldn't even *feel* that old biddy toothpick of yours." There was more laughter and backslapping, according to Wicker, at which point another black man called amiably, "Hey, Red. You the head man, when we gone chow down?" Just then, the train lurched; there was a general rush to the windows and doors. Wicker boldly punched the tall black sailor in the ribs and said, "Hey, Big Shot, where you from?" (Wicker 1975, pp. 157–59).

We can readily see how blacks' ability to withstand verbal abuse also featured in the interpretation of the black high school students (Scene 3) that the two students sent to the principal's office for fighting were "not going to do anything." We can also see how white interpretations of such verbal aggression were influenced by the conventions of verbal abuse that occur within white culture.

Wider Social Implications

The differing black and white conventions of aggressive behavior have other implications for black and white communication, with regard both to the timing and intensity of intervention by the dominant white society and to legal interpretations.

Black and White Communication

When opponents become angry and engage in verbal dispute, whites feel that they are reducing the danger of violence by keeping the antagonists apart. This is based on their view that struggle is basically divisive and that public arguments, if not stopped, will inevitably escalate into violence. Blacks, however, believe that personal differences can only be worked out by engaging in struggle, even if the arguments resulting from such an engagement become heated and abusive. To stop people from arguing is to deny the struggle and therefore the possibility of reconciling differences. Consequently blacks conceive the danger of violence as greater when people are not communicating with each other than when they are, no matter how loud, angry, or abusive their arguments may become. This general view is expressed in the statement of the black male faculty member in Scene 1: "You don't need to worry; I'm still talking. When I *stop* talking, then you might need to worry." This view is also expressed in the lyrics of one of Sarah Martin's songs:

Don't you turn your back on me,
'Cause it ain't never been your shoulder blades that I
   wanted to see.
When a lady's speaking don't you know your place?
How can I get results if I can't see your face?
[In Charters 1963, p. 84]

One example of the danger of noncommunication was reported by Joan McCarty. She told me that two close friends were having a number of personal problems and were arguing constantly. Finally, one person stopped talking to the other. The second person, after repeated attempts to continue communication, broke all the windows of the other's car. McCarty felt that if there had been *some* communication—arguing or whatever—this would not have happened.

Who will hit first? Logically, the person who feels more threatened, who believes that violence is imminent, would strike first, viewing the situation as simply one of "getting them before they get you." And this is what occurs. Whites, attending to the intensity of the interaction and operating under the view that angry disputes cannot be contained at the verbal level, usually strike first, believing the situation to be out of control. Blacks, on the other hand, often consider such situations to be quite manageable and are thus surprised at such a white outburst, believing themselves that people are "only talking."

However, in an angry confrontation, blacks are watchful for movement and may thus interpret any ambiguous move as provocative, even though the intent behind the move may be innocent. In such situations, the probability is that blacks will hit first, believing that violence is imminent and that it is therefore important to get in the first blow. This is what happened in the Washington-Tomjanovich encounter.

The prescriptions for avoiding violence arising from a misunderstanding of different verbal conventions are clear. Whites need to learn that the more intense levels of black speech behavior are not per se intended to be provocative or threatening. Achieving this understanding is not easy for whites, especially when the blacks with whom they are trying to communicate become angry, but it is crucial that an attempt be made. Blacks, for their part, need to learn what effect their speech behavior is likely to have on whites, much as the black faculty member in Scene 1 did when he said, "You don't need to worry; I'm still talking." That his statement did not produce the desired result is beside the point; he made the attempt. Had it been met with greater understanding, the white faculty member would have been relieved— and she now knows that she *should* have been relieved.

Whites also need to become aware of the significance of making an ambiguous move during an argument with blacks. However innocent such a move might appear to them, they should clarify their intention at the same time; the move might have a provocative implication that they did not consider. This was Tomjanovich's mistake. If he was moving toward Washington to break up a fight, he should have declared openly what his intentions were, since the movement alone could also mean, as Washington interpreted it, that Tomjanovich was threatening to hit him instead of keeping matters from getting worse.

In this context, blacks need to understand that such an ambiguous move made by a white in an angry confrontation can be in fact innocent. Should one occur, they should point out its provocative implication and ask for a clarification—or, as in the bar room episode in "The Flying Saucer Song"—issue a warning about how such a move is being interpreted: "Now, listen. Don't you raise that glass, understand?"

Many blacks have learned to clarify the significance of their own movements in tense situations. Richard Pryor (1979) has a satiric routine involving being stopped for a traffic violation by a police officer. Since the police, like blacks, are taught to be alert to any movement that might threaten their safety, Pryor gives the police officer very loud and explicit explanations of each move that he makes, in order to offset any possible misinterpretation: "I am reaching into my pocket for my license, 'cause I don't want to be no motherfucking accident."

Social Intervention

In the larger social context, the dominant white interpretation of verbal aggression and posturing as "threatening" works to the disadvantage of blacks. It enables whites to initiate repressive measures and still believe that they are acting defensively, when in reality they are acting offensively.

Cynical law enforcement personnel especially make use of the prevailing social interpretation of black verbal aggression by acting offensively—with full knowledge that they are doing so—but attempting to present their repressive acts as legitimate by referring to the "threatening" language and posture of blacks, individual citizens as well as groups like the Black Panthers.

Historically, of course, the dominant society has moved in prematurely on blacks, acting repressively while claiming to be acting defensively, so this practice is not new. As a rule, in the past blacks were not even allowed to express and assert themselves to the extent that white cultural norms allow, let alone black ones. For this reason, blacks still *front* in the presence of whites by concealing their true opinion and beliefs, even suppressing anger where expressing it would involve social risk. The irony now is that, as blacks begin to experience a greater sense of freedom to express and assert themselves publicly according to black cultural norms, they find themselves vulnerable again to whites who consider such behavior excessively emotional and provocative and to which they respond with incomprehension or violence.

Legal Interpretations

When white cultural norms alone influence the interpretation of words, behavior, and events, the probability of social injustice in cases involving culturally disparate groups obviously increases. This is clearly true of legal interpretations.

For example, both "fighting words" and "incitement to riot" statutes make a presumption about the capacity of the "average addressee" or "average citizen" to endure or withstand verbal abuse and calls to action. In doing so they presume that this capacity is common to all American citizens. Supreme Court Justice Powell, in *Lewis* v. *City of New Orleans,* admitted the possibility of cultural variation in this regard only with respect to the police:

> If these words had been addressed by one citizen to another face to face and in a hostile manner, I would have no doubt that they would be "fighting words." But the situation may be different where such words are addressed to a police officer trained to exercise a higher degree of restraint than the average citizen. [In Haiman 1972, p. 25]

But as we have seen here, the different conventions of aggressive speech behavior have developed among blacks a greater capacity to withstand verbal abuse. This would also qualify them as possessing "a higher degree of restraint than the average citizen." These and other conventions have also developed a greater ability among blacks to control the emotionally charged presentations of black speakers. Consequently those transactions that the "average citizen" might regard as inflammable or "inciteful" blacks may well consider to be quite manageable.

Taking Cultural Variation into Account

The white jurors in Scene 2 were willing to take into account what the various statutes defining "fighting words," "conspiracy," and "incitement to riot" presently do not—the possibility of different conventions of aggressive language in use in the black and white communities. Moreover, they were also willing to concede the superior qualifications of the black jurors to interpret the statements made in the Black Panther literature and so to agree to find the defendant innocent of "conspiracy."

But can we rely upon jurors always being more enlightened than the law? What if the jury had been all white, or even predominantly white, causing the black cultural view to be excluded? Would the Panther have been convicted of the charge of conspiracy?

Clearly, the notion that American society is "culturally pluralistic" is an impotent one if it merely *acknowledges* that people of different groups have different cultural patterns and perspectives. A culturally pluralistic society must find ways to *incorporate* these differences into the system, so that they can also influence the formation of social policy, social intervention, and the social interpretation of behavior and events.

Four

Boasting and Bragging

It all started twenty years past
The greatest of them all was born at last.
The very first words from his Louisville lips
"I'm pretty as a picture, and there's
*   no one I can't whip."*

Muhammad Ali, "Feats of Clay"

Blacks and whites generally agree that boasting and bragging refer to "vocal self-praise or claims to superiority over others" (*American College Dictionary*, 1947 ed., s.v. "boast"). But in other respects blacks and whites conceive of the behavior designated by these terms differently. In what ways and how these different conceptions affect black and white communication will be the focus of the present chapter.

Black Boasting

One characteristic always distinguishes black boasting. It is a source of humor. It is not intended to be taken seriously. Another characteristic, but not an invariant one, is its obvious exaggeration. No correlation between words and deeds need exist, nor is there any obligation on the part of the boaster to make them correspond. Thus boasts do not have to be proved. Boasters can exercise the full range of their comic inventiveness. For example, black *players* ("ladies' men") will say, "My rap is so strong, you won't know whether you coming or going," or "I got more women than Van Camp has pork and beans." Muhammad Ali boasts, "I can hit you before God gets the news" (1975, p. 295); and one black man nicknamed "Kid" said,

> I'm so fast. A girl told me one time, she said, "Kid, now if you can get some cock 'fore my mother get back home, and she's coming 'round the corner right now, you can have it." So I said, "Lay down." She layed down, I pushed the light switch, got undressed, jumped in bed, busted two nuts, got dressed and got outside the room before that room got dark. [In Abrahams 1964, p. 241]

Nor is black boasting exclusively a male activity. A black female boasted, "I can look through muddy water and spy dry land. I can look through any bush and spy my man." Another said, "If I tell you a hen dips snuff, look under his left wing and you'll find a can" (in Holt 1968, p. 1).

The same features mark black boasting in the West Indies. Karl Reisman reports from his fieldwork in Antigua, "Antiguan boasting is not the serious claim to serious accomplishment nor the non-humorous assertion by a hero which it might be death to challenge. The response to it almost always contains some appreciative laughter and shrieking" (1974b, p. 60). Roger Abrahams records the following rhyming boast from Tobago, in which the sexual feats of a man recently caught at illicit love making are publicly proclaimed and exaggerated. The singer assumes the role of the male fornicator.

> When I gi' she seven
> She t'ink she was in heaven.
> When I gi' she eight
> She lay down 'traight.
> When I gi' she nine
> She started to whine.
> When I gi' she ten
> Den my cock ben'. [Abrahams 1972a, p. 228]

Because black boasting is in essence humorous exaggeration, it does not always have to emphasize positive traits. Dick Gregory, when he was growing up, developed a kind of negative boasting—humorous exaggeration of insults that others directed at him—to make his peers laugh *with* him rather than at him. Thus, when one of his cohorts said, "Hey Gregory, get your ass over here. Want you to tell me and Herman how many kids sleep in your bed," Gregory replied, "Googobs of kids in my bed, man, when I get up to pee in the middle of the night gotta leave a bookmark so I don't lose my place" (1964, p. 41).

The foregoing examples reflect comic inventiveness. But boasts do not have to do this. They can be humorous in intent and effect even when they are no more than what Reisman calls "the making of one's noise" (1974b, p. 60). An example of this can be found in the boasting of Dallas Cowboy linebacker "Hollywood" Henderson: "I'm just the best linebacker in football. I'm the best linebacker ever to play football. I don't know why I'm not all-pro" (in Atkin 1979, p. 16).

Black Bragging

Unlike boasting, black bragging is a serious form of self-aggrandizement. Consequently there is an element of accountability present: claims have to be justified, whether they pertain to ability, possessions, or social status. But there is also a sense of appropriateness about bragging itself, apart from whether the deed proclaimed is demonstrable or whether a claim to possessions or social status can be validated. Here black etiquette distinguishes bragging about one's ability from bragging about one's possessions or social status.

Bragging about Ability

Blacks view bragging about one's ability negatively. As Muhammad Ali said, no one likes a braggart, and throughout his career Ali has shrewdly capitalized on this attitude as a negative attention-getting device to draw a crowd: "Before the fight, for the first time I'd talk openly about beating my opponent, telling not only him but everybody else, and the word got around that

'Cassius is bragging.' But when they came to the gym, they gave me all the attention I wanted'' (Ali 1975, p. 106). However, if the persons who are bragging are capable of demonstrating that they can do what they claim, blacks no longer consider it bragging (''No brag, just fact''). Moreover, there is then a marked positive shift in attitude toward that person. A nice example of this can be found in the Uncle Remus tale, ''Brother Rabbit Fools Brother Elephant and Brother Whale.'' Brother (''Buh'') Rabbit confronts Brother Whale and brags, ''Buh Whale, little as I is and big as you is I bet I could pull you out dat river.'' In response, Brother Whale scornfully says, ''Go along, Buh Rabbit. What kind of talk are you to talk. You couldn't move me in the river, scusin' for pullin me out.'' But after Brother Rabbit successfully pulls Brother Whale out of the river—assisted by an unwitting Brother Elephant—and comes to collect his bet, Brother Whale expresses the following admiration: ''Great shish, Buh Rabbit. You sure are an able little man'' (*Animal Tales Told in the Gullah Dialect* 1949). So Ali eventually came to be admired when he also began to demonstrate to the black community that he was ''The Greatest,'' in deeds as well as words.

Bragging about Possessions

Blacks also view bragging about one's possessions or one's social achievement or that of one's children negatively; they still consider it ''bragging,'' even though the claim may be true. This is in marked contrast to bragging about one's ability, and there are several reasons for the different attitude. One is that bragging about possessions or achievements offends blacks' basic sense of egalitarianism. They link bragging about how much money or how many cars a person has, or his social status, to being conceited or thinking himself better than the next person. When this sort of bragging occurs, therefore, it is denigrated. Faith Sloan, one of my black students, said, ''When one dude bragged about having a Cadillac, and it turned out to belong to his mother, I said, 'So what makes it yours?' ''

Bragging about possessions or social status also offends blacks because they feel that a black person's ability has had relatively little to do with his ''making it'' in American society, since blacks with ability historically have been rendered socially immobile or impotent by racism. Those who have achieved a measure of success in the world, relative to other blacks, are seen at best as having gotten the breaks; at worst, they are suspected of having made their way by sacrificing a dimension of their personal, cultural, or racial pride, often expressed as "forgetting where they came from" or "losing face."

This latter reason also explains why black entertainers and hustlers are often seen as career models for poor black urban youth. As Charles Keil notes, they are among the few black males who are viewed as wearing their black image in real comfort. Moreover, their material success is seen as a closer reflection of ability: these are "men who are clever and talented enough to be financially well off without working" (Keil 1966b, p. 20). Thus one black hustler told Julius Hudson, "I shall not work . . . . Dig, if you ever see me with a pick and shovel in my hand you'd better grab one too, because you'll know that I've struck gold" (Hudson 1972, p. 415).

Because of the high value blacks place on ability, they feel that ability should be given primary credit when it is the basis for a black person's success. Community blacks did not like it when Ernie Banks and Gale Sayers publicly attributed their success to the white owners of the Chicago Cubs and Chicago Bears, respectively, who "gave them the opportunity." Blacks said, "Their success was directly due to their ability. Wrigley and Halas just opened a door that had no business being closed to begin with."

We may ask why bragging about one's ability is acceptable but bragging about one's possessions or social status is not; that is, it is still considered "bragging" and negatively evaluated, even if shown to be true. Allen Harris thinks it has to do with the fact that possession and social status are not unique to a person. As he put it, "one Cadillac can be made to look like any other Cadillac, but nobody can duplicate Ali's punch."

Implicit in this remark is another dimension that explains the different attitude. That is, superior performance within a community context has a spiritually unifying and uplifting effect, one which, as Abrahams has observed, allows both the group and performing individuals to achieve a sense of fulfillment—the group "because it has come together and celebrated its overt values, and the individual because his abilities have been tested in a manner that allows him to achieve status" (Abrahams 1972b, p. 28). Bragging about possessions or social status, however, has no communal potential. Quite the contrary; the material or class values that it advances as criteria for individual achievement are seen by the community as socially divisive.

Campaigning

The distinction between black boasting and bragging tends to blur in such instances where bragging itself is not intended to be taken seriously but is part of a promotional effort to stir up interest in and excitement about an upcoming event—what Muhammad Ali called "campaigning" ("This ain't no jive, Henry Cooper will fall in five"). Here it combines the elements of boasting—"making one's noise"—with the elements of bragging, the need to demonstrate, at least in part, that one can do what one claims. Like Ali, "Hollywood" Henderson combined both elements. As he put it, "I put a lot of pressure on myself to see if I can play up to my mouth" (in Atkin 1979, p. 16).

White Boasting and Bragging

The 1947 edition of the *American College Dictionary* differentiates boasting and bragging, considering the latter more ostentatious and exaggerated than the former, and less justified with respect to the facts. Whites who presently distinguish the terms also feel that they are different in that one is more justified than the other, but they are not entirely in agreement with the dictionary editors that boasting is more justified and bragging "less well-founded"—some saw the terms in exactly the opposite way. Moreover, those who did distinguish the terms did not differentiate them behaviorally. Thus the only way they could tell if a person was boasting or bragging was to verify the claim afterward with respect to the facts. When they define bragging entirely in terms of boasting, the editors of the 1968 *Random House Dictionary* (s.v. "brag") seem to acknowledge both an inconsistency in general use of the terms and the loss of the behavioral contrast.

Boasting and Bragging about Ability

Whatever other distinctions whites make between boasting and bragging, they are uniformly in agreement that accountability with respect to the facts exists when a person boasts or brags. On proposed feats, boasts need to be proved within a certain period shortly after they have been made. Any attempt to forestall or avoid acting on a boast would invite ridicule, similar to that which might accompany an attempt to prove a boast that failed. Consequently, the rule among white male peers is, "Don't boast or brag unless and until you can make it good." This rule, establishing the accountability of deeds to words, has a historical precedent. A prototype can be found in *Beowulf:*

> The Danes had been served as he'd boasted he'd served them;
> Beowulf, a prince of the Geats, had killed Grendel.
> [*Beowulf* 1963, p. 49]

And of course there are numerous contemporary examples of the same perspective. Thus when Tom Landry, the white coach of the Dallas Cowboys, was asked whether he ever tried to muzzle "Hollywood" Henderson, his boasting black linebacker, he replied, "Not really, as long as he backs up what he says." To this, Henderson responded—reflecting the black view that boasts do not have to be proved—"That would be against my constitutional rights" (Pierson 1979, sec. 6, p. 2).

White boasting and bragging also contrasts with black practice with respect to the etiquette governing self-assertion. As white culture restricts individual self-assertion generally, it requires that individuals be governed by the norms of modesty when characterizing their performance, like "brushing off as routine an electrifying 75 yard dash through the enemy lines" (McDowell 1976, p. 16). White norms also regard congratulations and applause after an accomplishment as appropriate only when it comes from someone other than the performers themselves. For these reasons, whites tend to have a negative attitude toward boasting and bragging regardless of whether it is warranted, with respect to the facts. A case in point is that of chess champion Bobby Fischer, who has been criticized throughout his career for being cocky and brash about asserting his own preeminence, despite his consistent demonstration. Edmund Fuller represents this view in explaining his personal dislike of Muhammad Ali:

> Ali was the idol of millions, especially but not exclusively of blacks. Here I must confess that I have always, in the loose language of the anti-fan, "hated" him, always rooted for anyone against him. That was because I detested his persona, his strutting and chest beating, his doggerel predictions of knockout rounds, his ring clowning and "rope-a-dope" tricks, his bragging, "I'm the Greatest!"
> Mind you, it was not the man but the persona I hated . . . . But I felt no guilt; if it was his right to adopt that mask it was my right to loathe it, knowing his skills, aware that he was a great ring figure . . . . [Fuller 1978, p. 18]

Even if a person were to succeed in his boast, whites could always apply the pejorative term "show-off," thereby indicating that in white culture there is never an entirely "right" time to praise oneself for one's ability.

Black etiquette toward boasting and bragging is also consistent with more general attitudes governing self-assertion within black culture. Self-assertion is evaluated with respect to the content or objective of the presentation. Boasting is seen as a form of verbal entertainment. Were it to be criticized, therefore, it would be in the way a joke might be criticized: it was a bad joke, or it was the wrong time and place to tell it. Similarly, bragging would only be criticized if people could not accomplish what they claim to be able to do. If they can, blacks say, "It ain't even bragging."

As with other forms of individual self-assertion and display that constitute "showing off" in black culture—idiomatically referred to as "stylin' out," "showboating," "grannin'" (grandstanding)—there is also a right time for boasting and bragging to occur. Thus disapproving remarks that blacks might make in response to a person "showing off" should be construed as a comment on the intelligence or artfulness of the presentation, not, as with whites, on the fact of that person's self-assertion per se.

Bragging about Possessions or Social Achievement

The 1947 edition of the *American College Dictionary* defines boasting further as "speaking exaggeratedly *and objectionably,* esp. about oneself" (emphasis added). This definition agrees with the white cultural view offered here. However, in the later *Random House Dictionary,* boasting is defined as speaking "with exaggeration and pride, esp. about oneself or someone or something connected with oneself" (1968, s.v. "boast"). The phrase "and objectionably" is not included. I assume the reason for this change was that attitudes inconsistent with the white cultural view of the earlier edition were discovered. Black attitudes toward claims of superiority over others in terms of ability (e.g., "no competition") would justify dropping the phrase. But it is more likely that the phrase was dropped because the definition of boasting was extended to cover "someone or something connected with oneself," not only "oneself."

Other ethnic groups, in contrast to blacks, view bragging about social achievements positively. Thus Eastern European Jews often *kvell* ("swell with pride") or derive *naches* ("prideful pleasure") from the achievements of their children or grandchildren. Leo Rosten says, "Jewish parents are most energetic in *kvelling* over their children's endowments (real or illusory), achievements (major or minor), or praise from others (sincere or obligatory)" (Rosten 1970, p. 201). And considering the prestige that people acquire from having achieved the status of doctor, professor, or engineer among Jews, Germans, Ukrainians, Greeks, Poles, Lithuanians, etc., one gets a distinct sense that claims to individual superiority based upon educational and professional achievement are viewed positively in those groups. The attitude of blacks that regards such claims as "pretentious" is numerically overwhelmed.

Within the white cultural view represented here, attention is also directed toward one's possessions or social status, but less through direct verbal self-inflation than through socially significant forms of display: one's "exclusive" address; where, when, and how one goes on vacation; whether one has a nanny; or other kinds of conspicuous consumption (Wolfe 1966, pp. 236–44).

Cross-cultural Collisions

As might be expected, situations occur in which the different meanings and values that blacks and whites attach to boasting and bragging collide. An example was reported by Joan McCarty. It occurred in a television interview with some black basketball players and their white coach from Chicago's Morgan Park High School. The team had just won by one point a very tough championship basketball game. One of the main players of the team, asked to comment on their opponents, was serious at first, talking about "playing hard and matching us height for height," etc. However, he ended up with the exultant and self-congratulatory "But we were just too good for them!" At this point his teammates joined in a chorus, each one loudly assenting and "slapping five." McCarty said, "Even the black sports announcer started smiling at that." But it was also at this point that the white coach felt obliged to step in and, as McCarty said, "clean it up," by extending the customary white compliments and credits to a "defeated but valiant opponent."

Analysis

The coach interpreted (or at least responded to) the black team's boasting in accordance with white cultural norms. Within this framework, the teammates congratulating themselves on their achievement violated etiquette, specifically the demands of modesty that require performers to understate the value of their achievement if they are to talk about it at all. The black players did just the opposite. Moreover, since their claims to superiority were directly linked to a real accomplishment, they carried implications from the white perspective of "unsportsmanlike conduct": "rubbing it in" or gloating over the defeat of an adversary. This violated the white norm that one should be charitable to the opponent one has just defeated. Because of these violations, the white coach felt the need to step in and reestablish the dominance of white decorum rules.

Blacks, on the other hand, would see the players' claim to superiority as a source of humor. Hence the smile of the black sports announcer and the laughter of Joan McCarty, Allen Harris, and other blacks who watched the game. Their interpretation was based on the obvious irony of the boast—the win coming from a successful thirty-foot jump shot with one second left to play—as well as the exultation of the black players. Had the team won by twenty-five points, there would have been considerably less exultation, since the element of irony (luck or chance) would have been absent. Thus a statement like "We were just too good for them" in that situation would be a simple statement of fact. Blacks would not consider it to be bragging, as would whites, because it was true. It would not be boasting, because with the element of irony absent, the basis of humor underlying the players' simultaneous flaunting and mocking self-praise would be lost. The self-congratulation of the team might elicit admiration from blacks, as successful performances do, but hardly laughter.

If the team losing by one point were black, they would hardly be piqued by the boasting of the winning team, since the boasting would not be taken as serious. Moreover, the losing team would probably have done the same thing if they had won. If the losing team were white and interpreted the black players' boasting in terms of white cultural norms, they would probably be upset. On the other hand, if television commercials and programs are any indication—Matt Snell for Miller's Lite Beer, O. J. Simpson for Foster Grant, Gary Coleman of *Diff'rent Strokes*—the black conception of boasting is apparently becoming publicly understood. If this is the case, white players might also recognize and respond to black boasting as blacks do, interpreting it not as an unwarranted and uncouth claim to superiority but as humor: "the assertion of oneself, the making of one's noise, which depends not so much on the specific content of the boast as on the fact that it is made—loudly—at all" (Reisman 1974b, p. 60).

Five

Male and Female Interaction
The First Phase

In a recently desegregated high school, a black male student is charged by a white female student with "sexual assault." Upon investigating the charge, the principal learns that during the lunch break, the black student was standing with some of his black male friends when the white female walked by. As she passed him, he said, with obvious reference to her behind, "Shake that thang, baby." The white student continued walking and did not respond. After school another encounter took place. This time, as the white student walked by with a friend, the black student said, "Hey, baby, let me talk to you a minute!" As he said this, he left his group and placed his hand on her arm to direct her out of hearing range of his friends and hers. He then began to tell her how "fine" she looked, what a great "lover" he was, and how much he could "do" for her. She responded by pleading with him to let her alone, and she turned and walked away. Later the sexual assault charge was filed by the girl and her parents, her father in a rage at his daughter having been "insulted" and having "hands laid upon her." He demanded the black student's suspension from school.

When confronted with the charge, the black student said, "All I said was 'Shake that thang.' Now what the hell is wrong with that?" He also accused the white girl of "*wanting* me to talk to her," saying, "How come she stopped and didn't keep on walking?"

The principal, after listening to both sides, suspended the black student from school for three days, with the warning that he and his friends "had better keep away from white females, either on or off school grounds."

Similar incidents occur frequently in desegregated schools throughout the country. The charge of sexual assault brought by this white student is an unusual and extreme reaction, but the pattern of response is typical, including the disciplining of the black male student. The basis of the response of the white female and her parents—certainly its intensity—is undoubtedly rooted in unresolved conflicts regarding interracial sex in American society (see Day 1974 and Hernton 1966).

But it is also important to recognize that the white female's response pattern in this instance was only partially affected by the fact that the male was black, just as the pattern of behavior used by the black male had very little to do with the fact that the female was white. The behavior of the black man would have been much the same if the female had been black, just as the behavior of the white woman would have been much the same if the approach of the black man were used by a white man. This is because in black culture it is customary for black men to approach black women in a manner that openly expresses a sexual interest, while in white culture it is equally customary for "respectable" women to be offended by an approach that presumes sexual interest and availability. The basis of the conflict between the black male and white female, then, is cultural as well as racial. It is this cultural dimension that I wish to develop in this chapter.

Cultural Norms and Protocols

Both black and white cultural norms entitle men to express a sexual interest in women. Where the two cultures differ is in their acknowledgment that women are also entitled to express a sexual interest in men. White culture disallows this, or at least operates on the principle that women are not so entitled. Black culture, however, operates on the principle that women are.

Black Cultural Patterns

The black speech event called *rapping* reflects the black perspective. As a cultural mechanism, rapping allows a man to approach a woman, wherever the opportunity presents itself, and start to *rap to* or *hit on* her. An "opportunity" is typically a time and place where a man can talk to a woman without being intruded upon by others. Thus it can occur in a cocktail lounge, on the beach, on the street, in the park, at a party, or on the dance floor. Where talking is not possible, a man may indicate his sexual interest in a woman nonverbally, with what black men call a "silent rap" or "pimp eye." The purpose and motivation of rapping varies little. Men rap to women in the hope of getting sex. Sometimes men rap to exercise their verbal ability: sharpen their line or their wit or, as one black man remarked, to "deposit their image," to try to prove that they could "score" if they wanted to.

The topical content of raps can vary. But it is not unusual for men to declare their sexual interest and desires openly, comment directly on the sexually attractive features of females, or brag about their own sexual ability. The language itself may be explicit and direct or more subtle and metaphorical. But it is invariably sexual. "Street" or "storefront" raps tend to be sexually direct and explicit. Thus in one street rap a young man says to a woman of about twenty, walking by in tight shorts:

Male: What's happenin', fox?
Female: Nothing.
Male: You mean with all that you got ain't nothin' happenin'?
Female: Get lost nigger.
Male: Come here you funky bitch.
Female: What the hell do you want?
Male: I want some leg, baby. [Collins 1968, p. 3]

In one storefront at a Sunday afternoon "mini-skirt party," a "high gentleman, evidently excited by all the short skirts and legs on parade, announced to the entire gathering: 'Hey, all y'all pretty bitches. I got a numb member and it needs revivin'—right now'" (Young 1967, p. 3).

Blues lyrics also reflect this direct and explicit male sexual approach:

When you see me comin' mama, hang yo' draws on the line,
When you see me comin' mama, hang yo' draws on the line.
All I want is yo' behind.

But the use of sexual metaphors in the blues is perhaps more common. Thus, from a males blues singer:

She's got a sweet jelly, my woman's got a sweet jelly roll,
Yes she's got a sweet jelly, my woman's got a sweet jelly roll.
It takes her jelly to satisfy my soul.

And from female blues singer Ida Cox:

If he didn't like my potatoes, why did he dig so deep?
If he didn't like my potatoes, why did he dig so deep?
In his mama's potato patch, five and ten times a week.
[In Charters 1963, pp. 87, 90]

The approach of black men in cocktail lounges frequented by more middle-class blacks is less explicit but equally obvious in its sexual reference. One male's opening line was "Say, baby. Give me the keys to your pad. I want to play with your cat." Another said, "Hell baby, don't never give nothin' away. I'm buyin' all of it" (Young 1967, p. 3).

Black women's role and pattern of response to the rapping of black men is active and forceful, for in black culture traits like independence, aggressiveness, and sexual assertiveness are seen to be common to both males *and* females (Lewis 1975, p. 230). Likewise, women are free to express their own sexual interest in men. But of course a woman is not obliged to have such an interest in a man rapping to her simply because he proposes that she should. Collected examples of rapping, with female responses, indicate the variation one would expect. Men are either supported or rejected, in varying ways. In one form of support, the woman may express a reciprocal sexual interest in the man.

Thus to one man who said, "Mama, you sure a fine looking woman," the woman responded, "You looking pretty fine yourself!" Another took a similar remark as a simple compliment, which reaction can also indicate an absence of sexual interest while enabling a woman to avoid rejecting a man directly. In this instance the woman responded, "Why, thank you, you sure made my day," engaged in a few verbal pleasantries, and then left, saying, "I got to run, my kids are waiting, hope to see you again."

Direct rejection by women varies from a simple nonverbal put-down to a more forceful verbal insult. For example, when a group of males were looking at a group of females at the beach, one man said, "Man, they got fine foxes, all up in here." One of the females responded with an "evil" look. The man responded, "Baby, I don't mean no harm. Y'all all know you looking good anyway" (Collins 1968, p. 2; in this context, "up in here" means "excellent"; "evil" means "inhospitable," "cold," and "nasty"). But a man who was annoying a woman with his attention gave the following rap: "I may not be the man of yo' dreams on top, but you ain' never had no dream like the one I can give, 'cause I'm a lover." The woman answered, "Fuck you, nigger. You ain' shit, and you know *I* know" (Young 1967, p. 2).

In response to a rap, black women are not only as sexually assertive as black men; they are often equally verbally skilled, frequently *capping* a male rap with an effective retort of their own. In one example, a man coming from the bathroom forgot to zip his pants. An unescorted party of women kept watching him and laughing among themselves. The man's friends "hipped" him to what was going on. He then approached one woman and said, "Hey, baby, did you see that big black Cadillac with full tires— ready for action with nobody but you?" She responded, "No, motherfucker, but I saw a little gray Volkswagen with two flat tires" (Young 1967, p. 3).

Claudia Mitchell-Kernan gives an example of a more extended rap which occurred between her and a black man whom she encountered in a park with his friends while she was doing research:

Male: Mama, you sho is fine.
Mitchell-Kernan: That ain no way to talk to your mother.

Male: You married?

M-K: Um hm.

Male: Is your husband married?

M-K: Very.

At this point the conversation shifts, with Mitchell-Kernan explaining her research project to him. They talk about the project, then the man returns to his original rapping style:

Male: Baby, you a real scholar, I can tell you want to learn. Now if you'll just cooperate a li'l bit, I'll show you what a good teacher I am. But first we got to get into my area of expertise.

M-K: I may be wrong, but seems to me we already in your area of expertise.

Male: You ain' so bad yourself, girl. I ain't heard you stutter yet. You a li'l fixated on your subject though. I want to help a sweet thang like you all I can. I figure all that book learning you got must mean you been neglecting other areas of your education.

M-K: Why don't you let me point out where I can best use your help?

Male: Are you sho' you in the best position to know?

At this point the rapping exchange ends, with the male saying, "I'mo leave you alone, girl. Ask me what you want to know" (Mitchell-Kernan 1971, pp. 106–7).

One female response to the black male approach that men typically find unacceptable—especially when the rap is expressed as a compliment—is to ignore it. For a woman to do so often results in her being "loud-talked." Carolyn Jones, a black woman, reported that walking to church with her female friend, she passed a group of men, one of whom said, "Hey, foxes, you all sure do look fine. How you doing?" Jones responded, but her friend looked straight ahead and did not reply. This prompted the man to say, louder and directly to her, "Hey, baby, I said how you doing?" When she still did not respond, he said in an even louder voice, just as she was about to enter the church, "What's the matter? Don't you recognize me with my clothes on?"

Some black women have indicated that they respond to a rap basically to avoid being loud-talked. Others say that their response is based upon the kind of verbal approach used; they react to a more blatant sexual approach with an impatient "rolling of the eyes." Joan McCarty was walking with her young daughter when a man approached. Speaking to the daughter, he said, "I sure would have liked to make you with your mama"; then he looked at McCarty. She remarked on this afterward, "It's obvious by this that the man was not truly interested in me. I'll raise his consciousness!"

Despite the different attitudes that black women express toward what they consider to be an acceptable or unacceptable rap, they agree that they expect black men to rap and to be able to rap well. As McCarty put it, "The man's inability to come up with a decent rap indicates some kind of ineptness, which is often translated into sexual ineptness by black women."

White Cultural Patterns

The white male's sexual approach is guided by the general cultural view that there are two kinds of women: "good" and "bad." "Good" women are those who deny or conceal their sexual interest. These women are also careful about screening potential male suitors before meeting them. This screening serves two purposes. First, it increases the female's sexual protection by inviting the attention and concern of her family and friends and his. Hence, the man knows that if he makes improper sexual advances, his actions will be called into account. The second purpose of screening is to qualify men with respect to certain social criteria: occupation, education, income, ethnic background, religion, etc., establishing them as suitable or unsuitable marriage material and indicating that the woman is discriminating with regard to males: she is someone who will not go with "just any man." Good women are also assessed with regard to "feminine" character traits. Where men are seen as independent, aggressive, and sexually assertive, good women are seen as dependent, passive, and sexually receptive. Women become "bad" or "less respectable" to the extent that they admit to having a sexual interest, meet men without screening them first, or become "masculine" in character—independent, aggressive, and sexually assertive.

The verbal approach of white men corresponds to the general cultural norms that women are expected to deny or conceal their sexual interest and that any approach that would force a woman to acknowledge such an interest would be rejected, along with the man making it. Thus white men couch messages implying sexual interest in the form of innocent requests or offers. They ask women to have a cup of coffee or offer to give them a lift home. Used in this way, such messages become ambiguous. They are nonsexual on the surface, but the offer and its acceptance have sexual implications, especially if such offers and acceptances increase in frequency and acceptance would lead to a situation where the opportunity to have sex is present.

The interests of white men and women are only partially served by the ambiguity. It allows them to renege at any time before sexual moves actually occur. The sexual implication of a series of offers and acceptances can be repudiated by an insistence that the alleged reason for being together—the lift home, the woman's invitation to a cup of coffee in her place afterward, was the *only* meaning that either of them intended. Publicly, however, the ambiguity often does them a disservice. For example, it may not allow them simply to have a conversation over a drink in a public lounge without outsiders—or one of the couple—attaching sexual significance to it.

Inferring Sexual Outcomes

White male and female encounters acquire their sexual meaning circumstantially. Situational factors, such as how and where a woman allowed herself to be met, whether she agreed to be alone with a man, are significant in establishing the degree of likelihood that a sexual outcome will occur. Equally significant is reference to various male offers and female acceptances that cumulatively signify an investment of time, money, and attentive concern from which the male might hope to gain a sexual return.

Black male and female encounters acquire their sexual meaning through verbal negotiation. The man establishes his sexual interest at the outset by rapping, the woman by her initial agreement to interact with him further. Situational factors play no role in indicating the degree of likelihood of a sexual outcome. Thus a black man who met a black woman on the street or in a cocktail lounge would not feel that he had better prospects for succeeding sexually with her—because of where they met—than with a woman he met through a friend at a party. Nor could he assume that his chances of success were better because she was willing to be alone with him, although he might hope so. Sexual outcomes are transacted among blacks as initial sexual interest is indicated, namely, through open and direct verbal expression and negotiation. One young man who had just started to date a young woman confronted her with "Do you want me as much as I want you?" Upon receiving a nasty look as a response, he asked her half-joking and half-seriously, "Is it no for now or no forever?" (Collins 1968, p. 2).

In white culture, women who admit a general sexual interest in men fall into the "less respectable" category and are therefore seen as sexually available. White men are typically less respectful of such women. Consequently they are less patient and re-strained, less likely to take no for an answer in moving the course of the transaction to a sexual conclusion. Moreover, white men feel that women who verbally acknowledge a sexual interest as well as those who allow themselves to be "picked up" forfeit some of their prerogative of discrimination with regard to men. White men feel these women will sleep with any man and therefore will not refuse them.

In black culture, it would be wrong to infer female sexual availability simply from an expression of sexual interest or sexual assertiveness, since the culture presumes that *all* women have a general sexual interest in men and are sexually assertive. Black women are not viewed as more or less "respectable" on the basis of these criteria. It would also be wrong to infer female sexual availability simply because the black male approach presumes it. As shown in the rapping examples given above, such as the one reported by Mitchell-Kernan, a black woman loses none of her prerogatives of discrimination among men or refusal of a male proposal of a sexual encounter. As the examples above show, black men make their sexually audacious proposals but do not thereby deny females their right of refusal. For while black men may presume all women to be sexually available *generally*, they do not assume that these women will be sexually available to them *specifically*. Male raps are proposals, not non-negotiable commands. Nor are black men necessarily offended when women refuse them, accustomed as they are to hearing many more rejections to their proposals than acceptances. They might be offended by the way they are rejected, if they are degraded or ignored entirely, but not by the rejection itself.

Cross-cultural Interpretations and Conflicts

Both white and black males and females interpret each others' behavior in accordance with the meaning and value that behavior has within their own culture. In an encounter like the one described at the beginning of this chapter, a white female will correlate the sexual approach of a black male with that of white males in her culture who make "indecent" proposals and try to pick her up. Consequently she will not respond to him, for she feels that to do so would be interpreted as a sign of encouragement and would place her in the "less respectable" female category. She would be subjected to the pressures such women often experience when they respond to sexual proposals in white culture. In this instance, she would regard the explicit sexual content of the black male's rap as even more disconcerting because it would force her to confront the sexual intent behind his remark directly; whereas in white "pick-up" situations, sexual intent is often hidden behind an apparently innocent offer of help such as a lift. Tactically, this allows the female to deny the underlying sexual intent by refusing the offer. It also allows her to deny or conceal any sexual interest on her part in doing so, thereby permitting her to keep her image of respectability intact. But the obvious sexual content of the black male rap, which *presumes* general female sexual interest and availability, defines the situation as one in which the female is given *only* the option of rejecting the individual male—as in black culture—not the option of denying the presumption of general female availability underlying his approach.

A white female will also be disturbed by what she perceives to be a mismatch in the situation. The black male presents his rap in a verbally skillful, assertive manner, accustomed as he is to interacting with black females who are also verbally skillful and assertive. But the white female has been brought up in a culture that teaches women to be passive and sexually receptive vis-à-vis men and to rely on them, rather than on themselves, for sexual protection. In addition, she does not regard herself as especially skilled in repartee. Consequently, she believes herself unable to manage the kind of self-assertion or verbal skill that she feels is necessary to achieve parity in the situation. She may also be handicapped by norms of politeness that make her reluctant to assert herself when that might also hurt another person's feelings. Thus she will conclude that the only tactics available to her are to ignore the approach or, if that is not possible, to plead with the black man to let her alone.

But the white female's assessment of the potency of the black male's approach is an exaggerated one. So, consequently, is her estimation of the level of self-assertion she would need to create a dynamic balance in the situation. Black men do not draw the same conclusions as white men from the response of women to their sexual approaches. For one thing, because a sexual approach does not violate black cultural norms with regard to female sexual interest, black men do not consider such an approach "indecent," whereas white men do. Where women will lose respect in the eyes of white men by their response, they will not in the eyes of black men. Second, a black man does not infer that a woman is sexually available to him specifically, merely because she admits to having a general sexual interest or allows an approach that presumes that she has. To white men, such an admission would imply sexual promiscuity and immediate sexual availability. Finally, a black man does not infer anything sexual from the circumstances surrounding his meeting with a woman. The term "pick-up" has no special significance for him, because in black culture all women can be met in this fashion. The treatment that a white woman would receive in this situation would be the same as that given to a black woman, which is considerably more respectful and considerate than the way white men treat women whom they regard as falling in the "less respectable" category.

From the black male's perspective, neither of the responses white females typically use to respond to their rap is appropriate. For example, black men consider it rude to snub or ignore a friendly greeting or compliment. Black women who do so are seen as *saditty* or accused of "having an attitude," thinking themselves better than other people. Viewing a lack of response as arrogance, black men often retaliate by "loud-talking" them. However, black men also consider the pleading and helpless posture that a white female might assume entirely inappropriate as a response, for it implies an element of danger in the situation. A black male who raps does not intend sexual assault or rape, as some white women have supposed. Rapping is, after all, a verbal approach, not a physical one: audacious, to be sure, and perhaps offensive to women who do not want their sexual interest or availability presumed. But it is not dangerous. For a white female to suggest the opposite by a pleading response, however, often creates a real risk or danger of some form of punishment for the black man. In the example of the two students, it was a three-day suspension. At other times and places it has led to a man's loss of employment, bodily injury, or even death.

A suitable response for a white woman who did not wish to be bothered would be to interpret the rap as a simple compliment. Since the opening line of a rap often shows sexual approval, it is usually possible to do this. This may also entail having to engage in conversation a little while longer to satisfy the requirements of politeness, but after doing so it would be perfectly appropriate to make an excuse to leave.

Another response would be to consider the rap as a form of verbal play: entertainment, like boasting or bragging. Thus it would be appropriate to comment on the artfulness of the rap itself, or the absence of artfulness, as black women also do. One black male rapped the following to a woman at a party: "Damn, baby, you got what every man dreams of but what few men get." He was met with the reply, "You better tighten up your game cause your sound is sho nuff weak" (Collins 1968, p. 5). It may be possible in this way not to respond directly to the sexual intent behind the rap at all. One white woman effectively used the following: "It's a great rap, and I'm sure it'll work on a lot of women, but I've got all the men I can handle right now."

Of course if a white woman were offended by an approach that, as one woman said, "left no doubt at all what that man wanted from me," it is also perfectly acceptable to be direct in saying so, as black women do. As Joan McCarty said, "black women are beginning to just be up front and tell men that if they can't come to them better in the street than in the obviously sexual manner, they can just shut up.''

White Males and Black Females

Black women have reported that they often find it difficult to detect when white men are hitting on them or not, even though they suspect on general principles that sex is what men usually have in mind. The reason for this difficulty can be seen from the discussion above. White men and women communicate sexual intent circumstantially. Black men and women are verbally explicit. Conflict between white men and black women therefore occurs because white men think that the sexual connotation of their encounter has been firmly established by a series of offers and acceptances, whereas black women think the opposite, because the subject itself was never directly brought up.

Invariably, a black woman is later surprised when a white man starts to act on his presumption, asking him what she did that led him to believe that she would be interested in him. He in turn is also surprised by her rejection and her surprise, but he is also chagrined by being, as he sees it, deliberately deceived. The attitudes of both can be directly traced to different cultural understandings of how male and female encounters can generally be expected to unfold.

A more serious problem for black women is white men's inference of sexual promiscuity, based on their observation of black women who allow themselves to be picked up, who admit having a sexual interest, and who allow a male approach that is obviously sexual and which presumes their sexual availability. This kind of approach and response in white culture invariably leads to a sexual outcome. What whites miss, of course, is that black men do not regard such actions as making a sexual outcome anything more than problematical.

White Males and Black Males

Conflict between white and black males arises as a result of different cultural assumptions about female availability. Thus in one office a white man objected to a black man trying to hit on a white woman in the office not so much because of interracial prejudices but because he had an interest in the woman himself. Moreover, he had let this be known among the other men in the office, and he expected them to keep away from her while he tried to win her over, which the other white men in the office did. The black man, however, did not accept the white man's preemptive claim, since the woman indicated to him that she was not interested in the white man. Until she said otherwise, he felt anyone had the right to hit on her.

The basis of the conflict between the two men is cultural. Both black and white cultures acknowledge that it is ultimately the woman who chooses the man. But in white culture, the man hopes to win the woman by restricting the number of men who have access to her, thus limiting her choice and thereby increasing his own chances of being selected. A rule operating in the group I grew up with said that if one of us indicated that he "liked" a particular female, no one else in the group could say he "liked" her also. The declaration of intent was equivalent to staking a claim, which other males were expected to honor. Without any action on her part, the female became a closed territorial preserve to which only that male could gain access who had a preemptive claim conceded by other males.

Within black culture, the rules of rapping maintain that a woman can be approached and hit on at any time and place. Theoretically this places no restrictions on access to women, and in practice it is not unusual for a woman to be approached by different, men during the course of a day, especially if she is attractive. And black men recognize and expect that this will happen. As one man put it with regard to his woman friend, "I can't keep her in a cage, and I know I'm not going to be with her all the time." Thus it is not unusual for a black man to leave the woman he is with for a moment to go to the washroom or to the bar to buy drinks and return to see another man talking to her. This is not to say that some black men might not try to restrict access to their women in some way. However, without the cooperation of other men, this is difficult to accomplish, and the cultural rule that makes women generally accessible works against this possibility. In effect, black culture recognizes that the appropriate person to restrict access to a woman is the woman herself. This is why the black man in the office did not cooperate with the white man who tried to claim the woman preemptively: the woman herself indicated that she was not interested. Of course the black man also viewed the white man's preemptive move as a way to get rid of the competition without having to beat it, which he also considered devious.

Different cultural assumptions also affect the attitudes that men take toward other men trying to hit on their women friends. Because they try to restrict male access to a woman, white men generally see other men talking to their women friends as an immediate threat. A black man does not, rather letting his reaction to the situation depend upon the response that his woman friend makes to the second man. There is another cultural dimension operating here, too. Recognizing that it is women who select men, and that men are granted unrestricted access to women to make their presentations, black men understand that their ultimate success with women depends upon their rap being better than that of other men. For black men this becomes the challenge. The game is not only to win the woman over but to do so by competing with other men. The value of the prize is based in part on the number of others who want it. Thus beautiful women are sought after by black men not only for the value of their beauty but because they are sought after by other men. To succeed in winning such a woman is public proof that a man has beat out the competition. For some men this is not only one of their main satisfactions but one of their principal motivations as well. As Allen Harris points out, some black men become interested only when *other* men become interested. The white male mode that attempts to preclude other male competition works directly against the satisfactions that black men hope to realize in allowing competition and then trying to beat it.

Six

Truth and Consequences

Accusations and
Denials

    Accusations or allegations like "Men are sexists" or "White people are racists" are understood by white people to be categorical; all individuals who fit the generic criteria of "men" and "white people" feel themselves accused, whether they are guilty or not. Consequently, if those making the statement do not intend it to be all inclusive, they are expected to qualify the statement at the outset. Responsibility for statements of this type—their accuracy and the extent of their application— appropriately belongs to the person making it.

Among blacks, accusations or allegations of the foregoing kind are general rather than categorical; they are not intended to be all inclusive. Furthermore, the determination of who is to be included is not the responsibility of the person making the statement but of those whom the statement might conceivably describe. The applicable black rule is "If the shoe fits, wear it." Thus, to a preacher's sermon about "husbands gettin' money and ain't comin' home wit it," or "wives talkin' about I love you and not having no dinner ready when the man comes home from a hard day's work, and *he* got to wait" (Holt 1972b, pp. 191–92), only those husbands and wives about whom the allegation is true should feel accused. Those who fit the generic criteria of "husbands" or "wives" but regard themselves as innocent should instead apply the individual exclusion rule "He ain't talkin' to me."

Expressed metaphorically, the white perspective holds that the person shooting the arrow is expected to aim carefully and to assume full responsibility for all the targets that are hit, both intended and inadvertent. In the black perspective, the person shooting the arrow is responsible only for its general direction, not for the target the arrow hits, since it is the target that actually guides the arrow home.

Because *all* whites who fit the generic criteria feel themselves accused—not just those who are guilty—those who regard themselves as innocent will demand redress from the accuser, such as an after-the-fact qualification and, depending upon the seriousness of the allegation, an apology. If the accuser is white, he will understand the cultural conventions that make him responsible. Even if he chooses not to qualify the statement or allow personal dispensations, he will still understand why he is being asked to make them.

Within the black cultural perspective, however, there can be no inadvertent hits; for people to admit that they feel accused is, by that fact alone, to acknowledge their guilt.

These two views invariably clash in black and white contexts where blacks are making general statements about white people. Those whites who fit the generic criteria but consider themselves innocent will feel accused and will protest, "I'm not like that," in the hope of gaining an after-the-fact qualification or personal exemption. But typically they will not get it, because blacks do not consider the assignment of guilt to be the responsibility of the accuser. Moreover, because they have admitted that they feel accused, those whites will be considered guilty by blacks, notwithstanding their protestation of innocence.

On the other hand, those whites who do *not* protest their innocence are likely to be seen by blacks as *less* guilty since, by remaining silent, they do not acknowledge that they feel accused. Consequently blacks believe that these whites have applied the black individual exclusion rule "He ain't talkin' to me" and were thereby personally unaffected by the accusation. From the white perspective, these same whites will be seen as *more* guilty, since they also feel accused yet make no efforts to obtain a qualification or personal exemption.

An example from the literature illustrates this conflict well. Three white instructors, giving a course in black history to black students, were met with general condemnations of white society. Occasionally, the students would turn directly to the instructors with accusations of "deceit and evil intentions." This apparently provoked a heated and defensive response, for shortly afterward someone would admonish the instructors, "Cool it, man; we weren't talking about you." This admonition was an "apparent contradiction," since they interpreted the accusations against "whitey" or "white society" to include them. Blacks, however, saw such accusations as generally true but not categorically so. It was perfectly consistent for blacks to make such statements without intending them to apply specifically to those whites present. Of course, that the white instructors obtained such a dispensation indicates that they had already proved themselves in some way to the black students. Had they not, their defensive protestation would have been interpreted as a sign of guilt, and no exemptions would have been granted (Gregg, McCormack, and Pedersen 1972, p. 278).

Tom Wicker reflected the same view as that of the white instructors when he expressed surprise during the Attica rebellion: "When black orators like Florence spoke of unity in the yard but coupled this with blasts against 'The Man' or 'Whitey,' white inmates seemed to be cheering with the rest" (Wicker 1975, p. 304). But the black view that allows individuals to disassociate .

themselves from such accusations makes the behavior of the white inmates—influenced by black cultural norms—entirely consistent and comprehensible.

Signs of Guilt and Innocence

The black view that people who feel accused are guilty is based on the cultural belief that "only the truth hurts." When whites (or blacks) issue a vigorous and defensive denial—the kind that whites often use when they feel *falsely* accused—blacks consider this a confirmation of guilt since they believe that only the truth would have been able to produce a protest of such intensity. Claudia Mitchell-Kernan provides an example. It occurred when she was with two other black women, Mary and Barbara, in Barbara's home. Barbara had invited Mitchell-Kernan for dinner Saturday night, saying that she was going to cook chit'lins but then adding, rather jokingly, "Or are you one of those Negroes who don't eat chit'lins?" The person who responded to the remark, however, was Mary, who said indignantly,

> That's all I hear lately—soul food, soul food. If you say you don't eat it you get accused of being saditty. Well, I ate enough black-eyed peas and neckbones during the depression that I can't get too excited over it. I eat prime rib and T-bone because I like to, not because I'm trying to be white . . . .

This led Barbara to believe that Mary was the one who was sensitive to the implied accusation of being "assimilationist," for when she left, Barbara said, "Well, I wasn't signifying at her, but like I always say, if the shoe fits, wear it" (Mitchell-Kernan 1971, pp. 95–96).

Another example of this interpretation operating in black culture was given by Joan McCarty. Thinking back to her childhood, she remembered that when she and her brother and sisters were accused by their parents of having done something they should not have done, the first one to protest invariably was the one who had actually done it. And this was the way the protest was interpreted by the parents: "You sure talking fast, you must've done it." More generally, she said, "The first one who hollers they didn't do it is the one viewed as having done it." This view is also reflected in the proverb commonly heard among blacks, "If you throw a stone into a pack of dogs, the one who yelps is the one that got hit."

This pattern and perspective are also found in the West Indies. For example, in Barbados, *dropping remarks* occurs when an accusation is ostensibly made to a second party but is really intended for a third who is within earshot. The strategy for the party for whom the remark was intended, however, is *not* to respond, for "to assume a defensive posture would be tantamount to an admission.... To respond visibly to the *remark* at all is usually sufficient evidence that the ... effect ... of the *remark* has been felt" (Fisher 1976, p. 231).

Here we see what occurred in the situation reported by Mitchell-Kernan. Mary saw herself as the "intended" target, even though Barbara directed the remark at Mitchell-Kernan and indicated later that she was not signifying at Mary. By her response, Mary also indicated that Barbara's remark had been felt. We should note also the proverb from Jamaica which is almost identical to the one given above: "If you throw a stone in pig pen an de one that say 'quee, quee,' is him de stone hit." In Barbados, the idea is expressed proverbially as "Whoever de cap fit pull de string" (Fisher 1976, p. 234).

Whites respond in much the same way when accusations are specific or general. If they are innocent, they issue a vigorous and defensive protest and denial—especially if the charge is serious. If they are guilty and are not trying to pretend otherwise, their response is subdued and embarrassed. One company president counted on this response pattern when he accused a vice-president in charge of personnel with sleeping with one of the executive secretaries. The matter arose and required the president's intervention when all of the executive secretaries suddenly got a raise. Describing the thinking that led him to choose confrontation as the appropriate tactic, the president said,

> Suppose it were me. Suppose my boss called me in and told me I was fired and why. If I were innocent, I'd go off like a roman candle. If I were guilty, I'd sheepishly ask, "Who did you hear that story from?" That afternoon I called him in and told him. He lowered his eyes and asked, "Who told you that story?" [In Townsend 1970, pp. 98–99]

When they are guilty, blacks respond to specific and general accusations in a similar fashion. They reflect the fact that the accusations have struck home by becoming vigorously defensive in their denial. When they are innocent, however, their response to specific accusations is different. With general accusations no response is required or expected. Some blacks might say, "He ain't talking to me," but this is not obligatory. Not to respond either verbally or nonverbally is sufficient indication that one has not been touched, which is the customary sign of innocence here. Specific accusations do require a response, since the target at whom the accusation is aimed has been identified. Here blacks show their innocence by issuing a firm, nondefensive, deliberate denial and—where this is applicable—by offering to confront the person making the accusation directly.

An example of this pattern was reported by one of my students. It occurred in a residential school for delinquent girls. Two instructors, personal friends, had been discussing their weekend without realizing that they were being overheard by Rita, one of the girls. A few days later Rita confronted one of the women, Ms. Jackson, with some of the more intimate details of her weekend, claiming to have been told them by Ms. Redmond, Ms. Jackson's friend. Ms. Jackson was extremely upset with Ms. Redmond but got an opportunity to confront her only minutes before the time for a change of shifts:

Ms. J: How could you have sat down and discussed my business with these kids? I knew you were immature, but I didn't realize how bad off you are.

Ms. R: Girl, what are you talking about?

Ms. J: Don't tell me you didn't tell Rita about the other night, because she ran down everything to me.

Ms. R: Well, I didn't tell her nothing. What do you take me for, anyway?

Ms. J: I take you for a damn fool. Anytime a grown woman has to confide in a fourteen year old to discuss their social life . . . well . . . .

Ms. R: Where is Rita? Let's go back upstairs and see if she has the same story in front of me.

Ms. J: You go up there, I'm going home.

Ms. R: Well, fuck it, and you too.

Ms. J: Right, bitch. [In Williams 1976, pp. 14–15]

Ms. Redmond, innocent of the accusation made by Ms. Jackson and initially by Rita, denied the charge firmly ("Well, I didn't tell her nothing"), but without any defensiveness or loud protestation. Ms. Redmond also offered to let Ms. Jackson see her confront Rita, reflecting her confidence that Ms. Jackson would thereby be able to see for herself that she was telling the truth. That Ms. Jackson did not take Ms. Redmond up on the offer had more to do with her anger at that point and the awkwardness of having to involve Rita again—Ms. Jackson had denied everything that Rita had reported—than with Ms. Redmond's behavior, which from the black perspective was entirely appropriate in projecting innocence. Unlike whites, blacks do not go off "like a roman candle" when confronted with false accusations.

For this reason, whites often see blacks as guilty when they are not. Black students have often reported handing a paper in to a white instructor who later questioned them to ascertain whether they had in fact written it themselves, the quality of the paper being better than the instructor expected. Despite the fact that they had written the paper, the white instructor refused to give them credit. In discussing this situation with white high school teachers at a workshop, I learned that this was a frequent occurrence. A paper was not accepted because a teacher felt the black student's response was unconvincing. Several admitted that, had the student been more forceful in claiming that he had done the paper or in protesting against the implication that he did not do it, they might have believed him. But of course, from the black students' perspective, a more forceful and defensive response would have meant that the teacher's implicit accusation of plagiarism was accurate.

Other areas of black culture also reflect the black perspective revealed here. For example, William Labov (1972b, p. 334) noted that, in the verbal insult game of sounding, to deny, mitigate, or excuse a sound (verbal insult) is to admit that the accusation is true. Thus, when David, a member of the Thunderbirds, a Harlem, N.Y., gang whose speech behavior Labov studied, hits on a real failing of Boot's stepfather ("Least my father don't be up there talking uh-uh-uh-uh-uh-uh-!'') Boot responds to it and thereby concedes it to be true (''Uh—so my father talks stutter talk what it mean?''). More important, Boot shows himself to be vulnerable to the accusation that his stepfather stutters, and he is forced to take a defensive (and losing) posture within the game. What he should have done, and what experienced sounders have learned, was to respond to a sound with another sound, regardless of the truthfulness of the remark. Offense is to be met with offense, not defense. Boot should have used the response he made next to maintain his offensive posture and still remain within the rules of the game: ''At least my father ain't got a gray head! His father got a big bald spot with a gray head right down there, and one long string....'' Within the framework of sounding, as elsewhere within black culture, a defensive protestation of an accusation communicates to others that a vulnerable part of the person's psyche has been touched, with the compelling implication that the accusation therefore must be true, for the culture holds that only the truth hurts.

Information as Property

Seven

Typically, whites begin conversations with people they are meeting for the first time by asking for information. New neighbors will inquire about each other's family situation: the number and ages of the children, whether they all live at home, where they go to school, what the parents do for a living, etc. In seeking this information they do not consider themselves prying, believing that such exchanges are part of what they call being "neighborly" or "sociable."

They display a similar inquisitiveness at social gatherings, when they attempt to locate individuals they are meeting for the first time within some social, educational, and professional network or context. These inquiries generally reflect the way whites make conversation and specifically denote their preoccupation with status and social advancement.

Blacks consider the inquisitiveness and probing that whites demonstrate in these contexts improper and intrusive. One reason for this is that they reject the primary value given to social considerations that these questions reflect. Blacks are principally person-oriented. Consequently, what matters first for them are those aspects of self that people actually show in face-to-face interaction: intelligence, wit, charm, sensitivity or, conversely, stupidity, hostility, intolerance, insensitivity, etc. Social information, such as what people do for a living, may never become a topic of conversation in a black social gathering. As Sheila Rush and Christine Clark have observed, for blacks "parties have meant fun, frivolity and casual conversation with friends and acquaintances. The social event as an extension of business, politics or work is essentially a white phenomenon" (1971, p. 32).

Another reason blacks consider such inquisitiveness to be improper is that they regard as private much of the personal information that whites—or members of other cultural groups—exchange in public. One black woman remarked to a Jewish friend, after hearing two Jewish women talking on a bus, "Your people don't care who knows their business." Blacks are generally guarded about what goes on in their personal lives, considering information for public consumption restricted to those attributes and abilities that individuals display as part of their general presentation of self, such as those enumerated above.

Other personal information which individuals would have to be told about in order to know blacks consider private and confidential. Because of this, they object when people try to make such information public, what blacks call "having their business put out on the street" or "put out on front street."

A third reason why blacks see such probing as intrusive is that they think that the disclosure of personal information should be entirely at the discretion of the person himself. Only he can appropriately instigate its disclosure.

For these latter two reasons blacks see direct questions as an especially inappropriate way of seeking personal information, since they shift the discretion concerning its disclosure from those individuals to whom it refers to those who want it. In doing so, such questions violate the black rule of etiquette that grants the owner of the information the sole prerogative of deciding whether, when, and to whom it should be disclosed. Direct questions can also place individuals in the position of being asked to reveal information that they do not wish to make public and, therefore, in the awkward position of having to lie or to tell their inquisitors their questions are presumptuous.

To avoid these situations, blacks often respond to direct requests for personal information with silence, thereby indicating to those asking the question that their probing is inappropriate. One black woman reported going to work after a domestic quarrel with a black eye. She noted that in the predominantly black office of sixty people, "only one person asked me what happened. All within earshot gave her disapproving looks. It was not necessary for me to reply. She walked away, clearly knowing she was out of line."

"Asking" for Personal Information

Because blacks regard direct questions as confrontational, intrusive, and presumptuous, they are virtually obliged to "ask" others for personal information in a way that avoids what black etiquette considers inappropriate. This can be done by *signifying*. Signifying in black usage generally means intending or implying more than one actually says. Within this general meaning, it also has several special meanings. Here signifying means simply to hint or let on that you want to know something. Thus a woman who wanted to know how the man she was dating earned his money might signify by saying that she certainly enjoyed all of those expensive places he was taking her to and that she hoped his "oil well" would keep on "pumping that oil." Note that signifying operates for the most part within the framework of black etiquette in keeping the discretion about the disclosure of personal information with the person to whom it refers. If he so chooses, the man here can ignore the hint. If he does, it usually means not that he did not pick up on what was wanted but that he decided that this was not the right time to disclose the information. But signifying does not keep entirely within the framework of black etiquette, in that it forces the issue somewhat. In an ideal situation, the disclosure of such information would be completely voluntary. But in allowing individuals to ignore a hint, signifying at least avoids the confrontation that is one of the chief reasons blacks consider direct questions to be so improper.

Individuals vary in how long they will wait for another person to reveal personal information in which they can be expected to have an interest. Joan McCarty reported that another woman she knew went with a man for an entire year without knowing how he earned his money. Nor did she make attempts to find out, saying that if he wanted her to know, he would tell her. McCarty thought that was being a little too patient, and that if it had been she, she would have tried to find out by dropping hints similar to those given above. If he refused to pick up on the hints, however, she said she would eventually ask him directly, since such information is important for any woman to know. But in doing so, McCarty said she would hint first and then try to play the confrontational aspects down by saying, "Oh, by the way, how *do* you earn your money?"

The use of direct questions for personal information between close friends and relatives is generally more permissible. But even here, for some blacks and for certain kinds of personal information, direct questions would be considered intrusive. Claudia Mitchell-Kernan provides a good example showing how even sisters use signifying to avoid the confrontation that direct questions tend to force. In the instance Mitchell-Kernan describes, a woman named Grace had become pregnant with her fifth child and was disgusted with herself as a result, believing four children to be a nice-sized family. She chose not to tell anyone when she found out she was pregnant. Her sister Rochelle came over to her house at a time when Grace had begun to show. But instead of asking her directly whether she was pregnant, Rochelle signified, "Girl, you sure do need to join the Metrecal for lunch bunch." Grace, still noncommittal, said, "Yea, I guess I am putting on a little weight," to which Rochelle replied, still signifying, "Now look here, girl, we both standing here soaking wet and you still trying to tell me it ain't raining."

Of course, because signifying forces the issue somewhat, the way it is done also has much to do with how it is received. Because of the artful way Rochelle chose to signify, Grace found it "highly amusing" instead of "insulting" (Mitchell-Kernan 1971, p. 105).

Direct Questions as a Way to "Front People Off"

Another reason why blacks consider it impolite to use direct questions to seek personal information is that such questions can also bear the implication of trying to "front someone off"; that is, trying to get an individual to divulge information that he would wish to keep private not only because it is personal, but also because it would be clearly embarrassing to him if such information were to become generally known.

I was inadvertently guilty of creating just such a situation when I asked a young black man named Calvin, whom I hardly knew, how he had hurt his eye. He had taken to wearing a patch over it since the last time I had seen him. Calvin, who was with a male friend at the time and in a public work setting, gave me a look that told me it was none of my business; moreover, it was probably information he would not want anyone to know. During the embarrassing pause in which Calvin searched for a reply, a friend of mine appeared and saved my tactlessness by saying, "Tell the truth, Calvin; you were giving your girl friend one last kiss good night when her garter snapped." The force and humor of the remark, coupled with the reaction of Calvin's friend, who cracked up over it, provided a sufficient distraction to relieve both Calvin and myself of the burden of having to deal with the impropriety of my direct question.

Blacks view direct questions that attempt to front people off, or would have the effect of doing so, as they do loud-talking. Both are seen as expressions of aggression and hostility, if done deliberately, or, if done inadvertently, a reflection of gross insensitivity or stupidity.

Loud-talking in the black community is used deliberately and publicly to divulge personal information that other individuals would not want to have known. The purpose of loud-talking is usually to try to get such individuals to do something they have resisted or would in all likelihood not be inclined to do. Thus a young black woman, bothered by the persistence of an older man at a party, loud-talked him (or fronted him off) by saying, "Mr. Williams, you are old enough to be my father. You ought to be ashamed of yourself" (Mitchell-Kernan 1971, p. 133). By loud-talking him, she hoped to use the public embarassment produced as additional leverage to force him to leave her alone. Another black woman used the same method to combat the racially hostile attitude of a white waitress in a restaurant. When she received her food, she picked up her plate and conspicuously walked off with it to a vacant table in another waitress's station, thereby forcing her new waitress and eventually the manager to ask her why she did so. Her explanation ultimately led to an apology from her original waitress, which is what she hoped to accomplish by fronting her off.

Blacks are especially sensitive to the possibility of fronting people off or being fronted off themselves. This was reported by one woman who was standing in a line when a white woman told her that a seam on the back of her dress was split "so loud that everyone could hear." She said that she "would rather have let the seam stay split than have the information made public like that." I asked her how a black woman would have communicated this information to her. She said that in fact it had happened to her, and the black woman did two things: she whispered, and she used language that further hid the fact from others who were within earshot:

A: You're busting through.
B: Front or back?
A: Back.
B: Thanks.

Similarly, in a cafeteria line, a black friend of mine kept others around us from knowing his financial situation by asking me, "You covered?" meaning "Do you have the money to pay for both of us?" By keeping his voice low and relying heavily on context to communicate his message, he showed his sensitivity about others becoming involved in his personal affairs—or mine—and the possibility of such information being used to front him off.

An appropriate way to "ask" someone publicly to talk about something personal, or to make him aware that you already know something, without fronting him off (or giving the impression that you are trying to do so), would be again to signify. This is what a black co-worker did upon Calvin's return to work after the latter had done some time in Chicago's Cook County Jail. He greeted him with, "Hey, man, saw you and B. B. King on TV." B. B. King had given a televised concert at the jail during the time Calvin was there. Of course, this method would be appropriate only between individuals who knew each other well. There is no acceptable approach for those who are not so familiar.

Direct Questions as a Form of Signifying

Another reason why blacks avoid direct questions is that such questions are often used to signify on someone in a special sense. Signifying is not always just hinting or letting on that one would be interested in knowing something. It can be used to imply something that is negative or accusatory. Thus it is signifying to say to a friend whose home you are visiting, "I see that you've got the furniture rearranged," if you also mean to imply that it has been too long a time since you were last invited over. It is also signifying to bring back a diet cola when your co-worker simply asked you for a "Coke." You are assumed to be implying by that move that the person could lose some weight.

Blacks often use direct questions in signifying. To ask someone where he bought the jacket he is wearing is to imply that he has poor taste in clothing. Similarly, to ask a woman who is displaying her new dress when she learned to sew is to imply shoddy workmanship. Among friends this kind of signifying is often done in fun. Outside of this circle, however, or where the motivation is not clear, such questions can be taken as a sign of aggression or hostility. This is the way a black woman reacted when a white co-worker kept asking her why she didn't wear a wedding band if she was married, even though the white woman might have seen her questioning as harmless teasing. Of course, because the white woman was also asking her where others could easily overhear, the question also had implications of an attempt to front the black woman off, as well as a more general preemption of what the black woman saw as her prerogative to determine whether, when, and to whom such information should be divulged.

Because of the special inference that blacks tend to draw from direct questions, instances often arise in which whites ask innocent questions that blacks "hear" as signifying. This happened when a white department head asked his black secretary about a report he had given her to type the day before. She interpreted his question to imply that she was being tardy in not having it already finished. Hence she protested, "I've been very busy." He, however, simply wanted to know when the report would be finished, so he responded, "I know you've been very busy, and I didn't expect you to have it finished already. I simply wanted to know *when* you thought it would be ready."

Similarly, I asked a black student whose performance I was watching at a rehearsal whether this was her first play. She answered, "Did it look like that up there?" interpreting my question as suggesting a lack of acting expertise. Actually her performance was excellent, and I had intended simply to seek information, which is the way whites typically make conversation with individuals they do not know well.

The same kind of misunderstanding can extend to declarative statements. Thus, when a white television studio technician told a group of black students waiting to use the studio, "As soon as you've finished eating your sandwiches, we can start taping," their black director replied jokingly, "Oh, that means you want us to get finished eating quick and get our asses in there." The technician replied, "No; if I wanted you to hurry up, I would have said so."

Probing and Black Social Vulnerability

Blacks resist information-seeking probes not simply for reasons of etiquette but because, as a minority group, they have been and continue to be vulnerable to the way such information might be interpreted and used. As Grace Holt says, it is not simply that direct questions or other kinds of probing are impolite; they may also be threatening (1972a, p. 55). It is at least as much for this reason as for the others enumerated above that census-taking, for example, has proved to be such a difficult enterprise in the black community. Joan McCarty, who worked on the 1970 census as an office and field census taker in Lawndale, on Chicago's west side, reported that the black people she visited remained suspicious and basically uncooperative. As she described it,

> kids used to run up the steps to tell their mothers that a new caseworker was in the building. I asked one man his wife's age.

He said that I should know better than to ask a lady's age. Often, even after they did cooperate, they would say, "I know you work for Public Aid anyway." Many would express concern as to how this information was to be used and whether the IRS could see these forms.

In addition, this attitude recurred despite the fact that, as a black woman who was also pregnant, her personal credibility as a fieldworker could not have been higher.

Whites typically miss this most powerful implication of their inquisitiveness: that a response to a direct question might well increase the social vulnerability of blacks and members of other minority groups. Holt chides teachers for being especially insensitive in this regard as they probe the most intimate details of the lives and relationships of black students: how many people live in the household, who eats what kind of food, where individuals sleep, whether the family receives welfare, and so on. Black students try to resist such probes with such minimal responses as "yes," "no," and "I don't know," giving the impression that they are answering directly but not actually doing so: what Holt calls satisfying the demands of courtesy—the need to reply—but withholding the requested information (1972a, p. 55). But this strategy also has a way of backfiring, as when teachers interpret minimal responses from students not as a form of social protection but as a sign of the students' lack of intelligence ("inability to answer the simplest questions") or verbal ability (see Labov 1972a, pp. 202–13).

Thus whichever way the black students choose to respond, they lose. Were blacks—as well as other socially vulnerable populations—better able to influence or control the way information about them is officially interpreted and used, this would not be the case.

Eight

The Force Field

The differing potencies of black and white public presentations are a regular cause of communicative conflict. Black presentations are emotionally intense, dynamic, and demonstrative; white presentations are more modest and emotionally restrained.

This difference is consistent with the pattern that has been discussed in previous chapters. Where whites use the relatively detached and unemotional *discussion* mode to engage an issue, blacks use the more emotionally intense and involving mode of *argument*. Where whites tend to *understate* their exceptional talents and abilities, blacks tend to *boast* about theirs. Where white men—meeting women for the first time—*defuse* the potency of their sexual messages by disguising their sexual content, black men make their sexual interest explicit and hope to *infuse* their presentations with sexual potency through artful, bold, and audacious sexual proposals.

In essence, all of the black speech acts and events that we have considered so far—argument, woofing, cursing, sounding, boasting, rapping, loud-talking—have animation and vitality as their key attributes. As Paul Carter Harrison has noted, "The word MUTHAFUKA, however profane, owns more force than the tentative invective of GOSH DAMN! when trying to harmonize the vitiating effects of a depressed mode" (1972, p. xix). One even might consider animation and vitality *necessary* attributes for these speech acts and events to qualify *as* black.

Blacks and whites also have conflicting attitudes on the appropriateness of more or less potent forms of expressive behavior. Blacks favor forceful outputs. Beth Day, a white anthropologist who worked among blacks in the South, reported that the friendships that she had been able to establish with some blacks were in part attributable to her vigorously expressive nonverbal behavior. Blacks told her, "You don't hold back from a handshake," "When you laugh you are not afraid to make a big noise," "Your smile is open, like a child's" (Day 1974, p. 186). Consistent with this view, blacks regard more subdued or restrained expressive outputs as "cold," "dead," or not "for real." Thus one black woman whose expressive behavior tends to be low-keyed said that she occasionally finds herself criticized by other blacks for "acting white," blacks typically associating unemotional and undemonstrative behavior with whites. As Kenneth Johnson notes, the black pejorative racial label "gray" characterizes the lifelessness that blacks see in whites' unimpassioned behavior (Johnson 1972, pp. 144–45). Whites, for their part, favor more modest and subdued outputs, regarding more forceful expressive behavior as "irresponsible" or in "bad taste." As a result, in contexts where white standards and prescriptions prevail, blacks often find their more intensely expressive behavior criticized as a result. Joan McCarty reported receiving such criticism some years ago while watching *Lysistrata* for the first time at the university theater. As she described it, she was laughing heartily, thoroughly enjoying the play's bawdiness and humor, when a white woman turned to her and said, "You are really outrageous!" McCarty, hurt by the remark, asked what was wrong. The white woman replied, "You are laughing *so* loud. I mean, come on! It's funny, but...." McCarty said, "Daag. It's a comedy. Ain't you supposed to laugh?" But as she reflected in her report of the incident, "that was just seen as inappropriate, rude behavior. I guess I was supposed to feel the laughter, but not express it, at least not in the way that I felt it."

Emotional Force

The animation and vitality of black expressive behavior is in part owing to the emotional force or spiritual energy that blacks habitually invest in their public presentations and the functional role that emotions play in realizing the goals of black interactions, activities, and events.

For example, a common goal of black cultural activities and events is the revitalization of energy through emotional and spiritual release. To achieve this, three elements are necessary: (1) a sufficiently powerful agent-stimulus to activate the emotional (spiritual) forces that the body has imprisoned, (2) a structure like song, dance, or drum that allows for the unrestricted expression of those forces that the agent-stimulus has aroused, and (3) a manner of participation that gives full value to the power of the agent-stimulus and to the individual's ability to receive and manipulate it. This manner of participation entails a mind/body involvement of considerable depth, what blacks call *getting down into* the mode through which emotional release and spiritual rejuvenation are effected. Harrison speaks of the "gut-rending song of the blues singer who virtually *gets down* into the mode of sadness, happy to be blue, so as to purge the soul of sorrow by dealing directly with the onus of his wretchedness" (1972, p. xx). Linda Wharton and Jack Daniel describe getting down at a black social gathering in which a lead couple—through the dance structure known as *solo and circle*—is called upon to improvise a basic dance step. This couple is then encouraged by others, who start clapping and yelling, "'Git down, baby! throw down! Oh, Lawd,' thus spurring the soloists on to unimagined spontaneous creativity." As Wharton and Daniel describe the event,

> Aunt Pewee, pushed further by the people and possibly the liquor too, has thrown off her shoes—ready to sho nuff git down!

James Brown is hitting loose boodie, and Pewee is gone, doing her thang. Now Aunt Bertha, who is dancing along with Pewee just lifted up her skirt slightly over her right knee exposing half of the left thigh. At this point she is ready to burn Pewee. Uncle John yells, "Look out now, move on over Pewee. Make room for Big Bert!" Suddenly just as Aunt Bertha hit her best lick, Pewee goes off, off into a frenzie, doing movements she didn't know she could do. Pewee went down to the floor, did her split, rolled over twice, and in one twirl spun around and stood straight on her toes. Aunt Bertha, as you would expect, sat down and everybody continued to party the night away. [1977, pp. 78–79]

The black cultural pattern of *call and response* is basic to black expressive behavior because it integrates all three elements of stimulus, structure, and manner of participation (response) into a working relationship with one another. Like solo and circle in dance, call and response embodies an interlocking and synergistic dimension, in which members of the group participate by adding their own voice to those of others, to serve both as counterpoint and counterforce, alternating stimulating others and receiving the stimulus of others until collective spiritual release and regeneration is achieved.

Within the more formal call and response structure, as in a black Baptist church service, the preacher is generally identified with the call, that is, the one who supplies the initial activating stimulus. But, as Geneva Smitherman has pointed out, the word force of the preacher that functions as the call in the church service is itself a *response* to an earlier call to preach (1977, p. 110). And it is from this spiritual connection to his own calling that the preacher derives a good measure of his word power to invoke (call) the spirit in others. The spiritual connection of the audience to the preacher and his call is shown by the emotional intensity of their response, which in turn spiritually binds the preacher to his audience and, in the energy that it transmits to the preacher, functions also as a further call to preach (Holt 1972b, p. 192). Within the reciprocal and interlocking call and response structure, each call is itself a response and each response a further activating call.

In secular performances, call and response also underlies *doing your thing,* which in black culture does not mean, as it has come to be translated in white culture, acting independently of the group. Rather, as Roger Abrahams has noted and as the dance example offered by Wharton and Daniel illustrates, doing your thing means asserting yourself *within* the group, such as entering into a performance by adding your voice to the ensemble, by playing off against others—competitively and cooperatively at the same time—as each instrument does in jazz (Abrahams 1976, p. 83). It is, as Harrison states, "an invitation to bring YOUR OWN THING into a complementary relationship with the mode, so that... all might benefit from its power" (1972, p. 73).

Blacks also incorporate call and response into their more casual, everyday expressive routines. Thus the rhythmic style of walking that blacks call *bopping* represents a feeling action response to impulses coming from within. Yet bopping also sets a tempo for others to play with, on, off of, or against: a *beat* to ignite their sensibilities and actions. When activated, these also serve in reciprocal fashion, to revitalize the initial rhythmic step that sets off the exchange. Likewise, the hand-to-hand exchange that blacks call *giving skin* is invigorated by its connection to inner impulses and feelings and one's spiritual connection with others in the group. The genuineness and strength of both connections act as a catalyst to ignite the sensibilities and actions of others who respond by giving skin in return (Cooke 1972, p. 42). The integrated structuring of elements within call and response means that giving is getting and getting giving, in a rhythmic, interlocking, escalating, synergistic go-round.

The development of blacks' capacity for intense and spontaneous emotional behavior occurs within the framework of patterns—like song, dance, drum, call and response, or simply the speech channel—that allow for or can be manipulated to accommodate, free and uninhibited emotional expressions. For example, the structure of call and response places the intervals for calls and responses very close together, thereby enabling feelings to be expressed at or near the moment they are being felt. One can even say that if the audience and performer are spiritually locked into the cadence of the call and response pattern, the impulses and their release will occur almost simultaneously. Nonetheless, one cannot just come in *any* time. One must "drop in" or "drop out," as Grace Holt has said, in such a way that will not interrupt the rhythmic interactive flow. The same is true of black musical performances. As Charles Keil puts it, feeling is engendered to the extent that the rhythms conflict with or exhibit the pulse without destroying it altogether. Consequently, entering any ongoing black performance and being considered *on* time, whether it be music, conversation, or argument, requires that individuals coming in keep "careful track of the pulse" (Holt 1972a, p. 67; Keil 1966a, p. 345).

Emotionally intense black responses also occur because there are no restrictions on how forceful emotions can be expressed. The only requirement here, perhaps, is that the level of expression of feelings genuinely reflects the intensity with which they are felt. An obviously exaggerated response would therefore probably be considered inappropriate. Understated or muted responses would, since they not only belie the potency of the spiritual invocation (call); they are also dysfunctional in working toward generating the kind of intense emotional drive and energy necessary to achieve spiritual release.

Responses are obligatory within the call and response pattern. Thus, while there is considerable variation in the *kinds* of responses that individuals may give, some response is nevertheless called for when the slot within the structure designates that it should occur. As Smitherman notes, about the only *incorrect* thing you can do is not to respond at all (1977, p. 108). The main function of responses is to sustain the spiritual connection between performers and their audience. But the nature of the response also communicates to performers how they are *getting over* (Daniel and Smitherman 1976, p. 47). When no response is forthcoming, blacks are doubly chagrined; they are denied the feedback which they habitually use and upon which they rely to assess and sustain their ongoing performance. Black performers have been known to criticize an audience for their non-participation, or the indifferent manner of their participation, as I saw one black singer comment upon to a black high school audience she was entertaining, for making her work up there on the stage "all by herself."

The habitual use of the call and response pattern in black everyday presentations has led to communicative conflict with whites, who do not use the pattern. As Smitherman points out, black speakers tend to infer from the absence of a response that the whites to whom they are speaking are not listening. White speakers tend to infer from various responses like "Dig it!" or "I hear you!" which blacks consider necessary and appropriate interpolations to an ongoing performance—like saying "uh-huh" periodically on the telephone to let the speaker on the other end know that you are still listening—that blacks are constantly *interrupting* them (Smitherman 1977, p. 118).

Emotional expressiveness has considerably less force and effect in white cultural activities and events, because white norms for proper participation require that individuals exercise greater emotional self-restraint. For example, even where whites are given some latitude for emotional expression, as is the case when they are members of an audience at concerts or plays, the intervals between times when emotions are aroused and when they can appropriately be expressed are much further apart than with black call and response. Far from enabling feelings to be expressed at or near the moment they are being felt, white protocol here obliges audience members to check their impulses and contain aroused feelings until the appropriate moment.

Furthermore, even when the authorized moment for the release of feelings comes, the level at which these may be expressed is to be determined principally not by the force of the feelings themselves—as at black performances—but by the norms that are embodied in the white concept of *good taste*, which have set ceilings on how intense expressive behavior may appropriately become (Slater 1976, pp. 114–15).

The protocol pertinent at such white performances as concerts or plays allows for some emotional display, however contained. But the norms governing proper participation in other white cultural activities and events hardly allow any, let alone emotional display of any intensity. For example, the engagement of individuals in public discussion of an issue, without having their rationality or emotional maturity called into question (as noted in chapter 2), requires that they also keep their emotions contained and relatively subdued. To engage in "polite conversation" requires that individuals keep emotions in check and avoid issues about which people are likely to have strong feelings. Like Trevor Pateman's "idle discourse," polite conversation is static rather than dynamic: "Once begun it aims only to stay where it is" (Pateman 1975, p. 40).

Other everyday public presentations are expected to be governed by the standards for "proper demeanor," which, as Erving Goffman notes, in white culture includes such attributes as modesty in claims regarding self and self-control over emotions (1967, p. 77). Note that "self-control" here should be understood as the ability of individuals to check impulses and contain feelings rather than, for example, to be able to manage them at more intense levels of expression or, as Philip Slater has observed, to be able to call upon a particular emotion when you want it (Slater 1976, p. 33).

Whites rely heavily upon the ability of individuals to exercise self-restraint in realizing the norms for proper social conduct in public contexts. But as a safeguard, they also invest individuals acting as *others* with the social right to intervene to restore a more subdued public tone should people, following their emotions, produce behavior that is too potently expressive. Note that this special right of others to intervene directly is restricted to containing or suppressing what white cultural norms have determined is unduly forceful assertive or expressive behavior. However, others are given no special social rights to *induce* more active or forceful behavior, as when muted participation or nonparticipation is dysfunctional, even to levels that white norms would consider appropriate. That is why, as I indicated in chapter 2, it is easier to suppress irresponsible self-assertion in the classroom than to overcome irresponsible nonassertion. White students will yield to intervention by others to produce the first result—conceding that others have a role as custodians of public order—but will not yield to intervention by others (black students or the instructor) to produce the second result, viewing the right to muted or nonparticipation to belong entirely to individuals themselves.

White culture also grants individuals acting as "others" an indirect role in working against more forceful expressive or assertive behavior. It does this by presuming the sensibilities of "others" to be susceptible and by the interactional rule that says that individuals should moderate the forcefulness of their behavior to the level that others can tolerate. Both the presumption and the rule are manifest in the caution that whites often express about not doing or saying anything that might "hurt other people's feelings."

Capacities

Whites' capacity for exercising emotional self-restraint is developed by the standards set for proper participation in white cultural activities and events in which emotional expression is seen as having little or no functional role. But this capacity for exercising emotional self-restraint operates effectively only when other people are also exercising emotional self-restraint, which is to say, when everyone cooperates in keeping the expressive intensity of public interaction low. It is a gentleman's agreement within white social circles that self-control over emotions should not be made more of an exercise than it already is. And to keep self-restraint from becoming too much of a strain, whites also choose outputs and environments that have low stimulus value, thereby minimizing their capacity to arouse and excite. As Slater notes, clothes should be drab and inconspicuous, colors of low intensity, sounds quiet, smells nonexistent, words emotionless (1976, p. 115). But these concerns and precautions also indicate that self-restraint can become too much of an exercise for whites when the level of interaction becomes expressively intense. This is because white culture develops controls to contain emotions, but few or no controls to manage them at more intense levels of expression. Rather, as pointed out in chapters 2 and 3, whites typically consider self-control over emotions to have broken down when such emotionally intense interaction occurs. And for them it has, which is one reason why others intervene when individuals begin to behave in a loud and emotional fashion.

This lack of control over emotions at more expressively intense levels also affects the capacity and willingness of whites to engage in spontaneous and intense emotional behavior. A lifetime of practicing emotional self-restraint enhances a capacity for such self-restraint, but it does not develop a reciprocal ability to *let go* emotionally, or confidence in one's ability to control the impact of intense emotions once they are expressed. This "incapacity" affects the way white actors project emotions on the stage. For example, Harrison notes that actors in the American theater operate under the concept of *affective memory*, which tries to recall emotional events in order to approximate the tensions that they had experienced and thereby produce a similar response. "However, as exercised, only the cerebral acquisition of the emotion is desired, rather than the full visceral response . . . . The exercise is designed merely to allow the actor to repeat the same emotion night after night." In the black theater one finds an *effective memory* working, one that produces "the truest emotional response in order that one might galvanize the collective consciousness." But this requires an ability to produce "real, spontaneously conceived emotions" that, Harrison notes, white actors avoid, "for fear of not being able to control the impact of them."

Blacks have lifelong experience engaging in cultural events in which their emotions have become aroused. This has developed in them the freedom to abandon themselves to the force of their feelings without fear of being unable to control their impact. Whites often consider such an abandonment to signify that the emotions are *out of control*. But they are not—at least not within the framework of ritualized expression. Rather, here blacks have transferred a measure of control from themselves to the feeling mode (sorrow, exultation, spirit possession) and to the cultural form (song, dance, greeting exchange, call and response) through which the emotions are released and within which they are also contained. As Harrison says, "an emotion is never out of control when it fits the modality it is released in," to which he adds, "Only when it is outside the mode, however benign or malignant, does the emotion seem peculiarly threatening or unintelligible" (Harrison 1972, p. 157).

Because whites do not have such an acquired sense—either from their own culture or from their knowledge of black or other cultures—that intensely expressed emotions can be contained by the mode through which they are released (such as those which blacks express in *argument*), they regard *all* emotional behavior as outside the mode and therefore "peculiarly threatening and unintelligible."

Interactional Roles and Responsibilities

The responsibility for realizing the appropriate emotional level in public interaction is one to be shared by individuals acting in response to their own feelings and individuals acting as "others." The nature of one's role and responsibility in this regard is determined by how intense emotional and expressive behavior can appropriately become in the two cultures.

For example, the desired emotional level in white social interaction is generally lower than an uninhibited expression of feelings would make it. Thus individuals acting in response to their own feelings are expected to exercise emotional self-restraint, and those individuals acting as "others" are given a preemptive role in seeing to it that expressed feelings do not exceed the level of intensity that the culture has designated as appropriate. On the other hand, the level of emotional intensity in black social interaction is at least equal to what an uninhibited expression of feelings would produce and frequently *greater* than what individuals happen to be generating at the time. Consequently, blacks acting as others often try to get some action going by spurring individuals acting in response to their own feelings to greater activity— *agitatin'*, Harrison calls it—thereby increasing the levels of emotional intensity being displayed and so satisfying the need of others for power, emotional excitement, and revitalization of energy (Harrison 1972, pp. 36–37). James Maryland's examples of signifying between Sweet Red and Black Power at a shoe-shine stand and between black teenagers at the "outpost" (chapter 3) illustrates well the agitating (signifying) role of others in this process.

Reciprocities

The relationship between the freedom (or capacity) of individuals to produce intense emotional behavior and their ability to receive and manipulate it is a reciprocal one. This is because the level of emotional intensity that individuals show is regulated in part by what they know or presume others are capable of withstanding. Conversely, the level of susceptibility of individual sensibilities is developed culturally by the intensity of the feelings they are accustomed to receiving.

Whites keep a lid on their more emotionally intense outputs in part because they presume that the capacity of other whites to receive and manipulate them is relatively low. Of course this also ensures that the capacity of whites to receive and manipulate more intense emotional outputs will *remain* low, precisely because more intense outputs are being withheld that would give whites the opportunity to become more acquainted with them—to give whites the sense that strong emotions *can* be contained by the mode through which they are released. Such release would help whites become more interpersonally effective in receiving and manipulating intense outputs.

Blacks' capacity to deal with intense emotional outputs is relatively greater than that of whites because blacks have greater experience of being confronted with them. Reciprocally, this capacity also gives blacks acting in response to their own feelings greater freedom to express them intensely, knowing that others have developed the capacity to receive them without becoming overwhelmed.

The actual level of tolerance that blacks and whites develop toward emotionally or expressively intense behavior is determined by the different cultural norms of how intense emotional and expressive behavior may become. Through the kinds of outputs they are respectively accustomed to receiving, black and white individual sensibilities internalize a sense of appropriateness which they then work to maintain. These cultural norms also define the respective patterns of accommodation. Whites want social interaction to operate at an emotionally subdued level. To realize this goal, they first establish the rule that expressive behavior shall be subdued, which develops sensibilities capable of tolerating only relatively subdued outputs. The white rule then establishes that individuals should let their more emotionally intense behavior be governed by what other people's sensibilities are capable of withstanding. Since others are only capable of receiving and manipulating comfortably outputs that are emotionally subdued, the rule hopes to ensure that outputs will remain subdued. Thus white sensibilities become adjunct regulatory agencies assisting the dominant social group in keeping social interaction low-keyed and public contexts relatively cool.

Black cultural norms desire levels of public interaction that are more emotionally intense. Consequently they allow individuals to express themselves at the level at which feelings are felt and accordingly oblige others to accommodate such outputs at the same level. In this way black sensibilities also function as adjunct regulatory agencies working to keep the level of social interaction vigorous and animated and public contexts relatively hot.

Tact
Doing unto Others

The white interaction rule that individuals should adjust the potency of their assertions and expressions to the level that others can withstand is incorporated in their general notion of showing consideration for other people's feelings. Yet it is also clear that individuals do not automatically qualify for consideration as "others." Rather, individuals win or forfeit consideration for their feelings in accordance with their behavior. Thus whites who do not moderate the potency of their self-assertions or expressions to the level that cultural norms have determined to be appropriate or that others can withstand are judged to have considered the feelings of others improperly. Consequently these individuals have forfeited consideration for themselves as "others." The social punishment for that is withdrawal by other people of consideration for their feelings.

We saw this in an earlier example in this chapter. The white woman considered herself entitled to tell McCarty that the latter's behavior during *Lysistrata* was "outrageous" because the white woman identified herself and other members of the audience as the "others" whose feelings McCarty had not considered with her loud laughter. The white woman considered that McCarty had thereby disqualified herself as an "other" and forfeited consideration by others of her own feelings. The white woman did not consider herself rude in criticizing McCarty as she did since, conventionally, one cannot be rude to people whose behavior has just disqualified them from consideration as "others."

However, it is also clear that the feelings of others for which whites generally show consideration are not active or expressive feelings. Rather, they are passive and consequently should more properly be regarded as *sensibilities* than *feelings*. This distinction is important, because active feelings—which is simply to say *feelings*—have no claim on other people's consideration in white social interaction. Quite the contrary: individuals whose feelings become active risk forfeiting consideration for themselves as "others," especially if these feelings become expressively intense or threaten to override established order and procedure.

The distinction between feelings and sensibilities also enables us to be more accurate in characterizing what happened in the cited incident during the play. The white woman did not regard McCarty's *feelings,* expressed by her loud laughter, as qualifying her for consideration as an "other." Rather, she saw the latter's behavior as a forfeit of consideration for herself as an "other" and therefore a forfeit as well of protection for her sensibilities which the white woman then considered herself entitled—even obligated—to punish as custodian of the public order and, perhaps, also as someone whose own sensibilities had been offended.

Of course McCarty did not consider her laughter inconsiderate of other people's sensibilities, since in black culture, feelings and emotions are seen as primary and independent forces. They are primary in that they are seen principally to motivate and guide black action and to serve as a reference to explain why individuals behave in the way that they do. They are independent in that blacks relinquish to feelings the freedom to exert their *own* will on their behavior, and, consequently, on whatever proceedings they happen to be engaging in at the time. Thus McCarty saw herself as behaving appropriately in giving full value to the force of her inner feelings by expressing them as they were felt, thereby also acknowledging their primary and independent status. Moreover, as already noted, other blacks regard the manifestation of the primary and independent force and effect of feelings *positively*– whether at the level of expression or motivation. When during his fieldwork in Antigua Karl Reisman asked Afro-Antiguans why people can fall asleep or shift subjects in the middle of sentences, the answers he received were usually given in terms of the person's feelings. "That's what he feels to do," which denoted for Reisman the strong value Afro-Antiguans "put on not constraining one's feelings by artificial structures." He concludes, "A very beautiful and subtle attention to the feelings of others is a marked feature of West Indian tact" (Reisman 1974b, p. 67). When blacks express their feelings or act otherwise in accordance with their feelings, not only do they not consider themselves doing something for which they might *risk* disqualification as others. They believe that they are acting in ways that have a *preemptive* claim on others' consideration and respect. McCarty saw not herself but the white woman in the theater as being "inconsiderate" of other people's feelings. As evidence she would offer not only her own sensibilities, which the white woman offended with her gratuitous remark, but also her own exuberant laughter, which others within her culture would respond to favorably and appreciatively.

White students in my classes do not usually understand how Afro-Antiguans are being *tactful* in their consideration of other people's feelings, from Reisman's description of their behavior. This is because they identify the "others" in Reisman's statement ("a very beautiful and subtle attention to the feelings of others") to be the people who were *listening* to those individuals who fell asleep and who were left hanging in mid-air as a result. They do not consider that the individuals who fell asleep might qualify as the "others" here, because whites show consideration for sensibilities, not feelings. Thus the feelings that prompted the individual Antiguans to fall asleep do not qualify, within the white conception of tact, for consideration from others; moreover, to the extent that they overrode established order and procedure, they would cause those individuals who acted in accordance with them also to forfeit consideration from others for themselves. Finally, because whites see feelings as sensibilities, they do not conceive that the feelings of others to which Afro-Antiguans were giving subtle attention were the sensibilities of those individuals who fell asleep. Again, according to the white cultural conception, these individuals forfeited consideration for their sensibilities because of their own lack of consideration for the sensibilities of those other individuals who were listening.

But of course the feelings of others which Afro-Antiguans were attending to were precisely those that prompted the individuals who shifted subject in the middle of a sentence to do so. Within the Afro-Antiguan and larger black conception of tact, individuals who express their feelings or act in accordance with their feelings continue to qualify as "others" in people's consideration: even preemptively so, given the primary status accorded to feelings within the culture. These feelings, as already noted, are also those whose determinative force—at the level of expression or motivation—white cultural patterns and norms work to preclude.

The white social interaction rule that grants individuals the right to claim consideration from others for their sensibilities, but not for their feelings, extends to interpersonal contexts. Here, whites have been taught that to act on behalf of their own feelings is unjustified if someone else's sensibilities might become offended as a result. So strongly ingrained is this rule that it has the force of a moral injunction. Rather than violate it and feel guilty or, as a further embarrassment, have to engage in repair work (apologies, expiation), whites will hold back what they truly feel, even if this will result in an injustice to their feelings or create for themselves an unwanted social situation. This often happens to whites, especially white women who have been socialized to be more acquiescent and less assertive than white men. I have already noted (in chap. 5) how this creates interpersonal difficulties for white women when confronted with the assertive raps of black men.

Whites are not simply being altruistic in placing the sensibilities of others before their own feelings. Whites, after all, are "others" in other people's consideration just as other people are "others" in theirs. The same rule that protects the sensibilities of others at the expense of one's own feelings also protects one's sensibilities at the expense of the feelings of others. Furthermore, because the rule has the force of a moral injunction, those who violate it not only risk incurring feelings of guilt but in effect grant others the opportunity to assault their sensibilities, since they will have forfeited consideration for themselves as an "other" as a result of not having properly considered (protected) the sensibilities of others. Moreover, others can now assault their sensibilities self-righteously, since such an assault is also considered proper social punishment for the rule being violated. Thus there are strong practical reasons also for whites to follow their rule. The weight given to protecting the sensibilities of others in white culture leaves individuals with little or no moral justification for acting in accordance with their own feelings.

The black social interaction rule that grants individuals the right to claim consideration from others for their feelings also extends to interpersonal contexts. And while sensibilities also have a moral claim on other people's consideration, feelings are seen to have a preemptive claim. The primary and independent status accorded feelings within the culture means that individuals must place their own feelings first—indeed are seen to have no other choice than to do so if they are to respond as a *total* person—even if other people's sensibilities might become offended in the process (Harrison 1972, p. 155). Of course this also means that blacks must come to grips with others also placing their own feelings first at the expense of *their* sensibilities.

The different relative weight that blacks and whites give to protecting feelings and sensibilities was brought into focus some years ago in my graduate course on interpersonal communication. As their final assignment, the students, eight black and fourteen white, were asked to confront other members of the class individually and comment on the projected image or communicative style that each had showed in class during the past term. Such an assignment meant that, if done candidly, student sensibilities might well become offended. As a result, several students expressed concern over how it should be carried out or even whether it should be done at all. In discussing these questions, their negotiation ultimately centered upon the issue of whether feelings or sensibilities should receive preemptive consideration: specifically, the rights of those students who had something to say and wanted to say it (whether others wanted to hear it or not) versus the rights of students not to hear what others might want to say about them, irrespective of how much others might want to tell them. The way the class divided on this issue was culturally revealing. Twelve of the fourteen white students argued for the rights of students *not* to hear what others might want to say to them—thus giving priority to the protection of individual sensibilities, those of others as well as their own, even if this might result in forfeiting their own chance to say what they felt. This group decided that they would comment on others only if other students gave them permission to do so. The eight black students and remaining two white students, on the other hand, argued for the rights of those students to express what they had to say about others even if the protection of all individual sensibilities would be forfeited in the process. On this last point, one black woman said, "I don't know about others, but if someone has something to say to me, I want to hear it."

Many other examples documenting this difference have subsequently occurred. One took place in a restaurant at lunch time. A black friend of mine had his pocket radio on at a moderately low volume when the white manager asked him to turn it off, as it bothered some of the other customers. My own white cultural orientation then was to see the sensibilities of others as deserving preemptive consideration, even if it should be at the expense of feelings—my own or those of others. My black friend, however, gave the feelings stimulated by the music greater value than I did. He lowered the radio's volume a bit to show consideration for other people's sensibilities, but he refused to turn it off altogether in consideration of his *own* feelings—as well as those of mine and several others who were also enjoying the music—much to the chagrin of the white manager.

From a white standpoint, the black cultural pattern that would withdraw protection for sensibilities to save feelings is insensitive and even cruel. But of course the white view is based on the assumption that individual sensibilities are quite fragile—thus others need to be vigilant in giving them special social protection. Also, the special social rights that white culture gives to others to protect individual self-esteem makes any violation of other sensibilities especially potent and sinful. Finally, whites see the black emotional response as too intense. This is true even if blacks have been provoked and are *reacting* to individuals who have just offended them and who, according to both black and white norms, would have forfeited their right to receive polite consideration for *their* sensibilities. Whites would still consider the black response an overreaction. They would wonder what horrendous offense the other person could have committed to deserve such an emotionally powerful retaliatory response. White sympathies will typically be with the person on the receiving end of such an exchange—almost without regard to provocation—rather than with the person asserting himself in such an intense manner.

From a black standpoint, individuals asserting themselves in accordance with their feelings are seen not as violating the sacred rights of others but, rather, as preserving the sacred rights of self, especially the sanctity of individual feelings and the primary and independent status that feelings have within the culture. With the shift in focus from *doing unto others* to *doing for oneself,* blacks can also act as their feelings direct without subsequent guilt. Of course they also do not consider the rights of others to be especially violable here, because they do not consider the sensibilities of others to be so fragile that they will be overwhelmed by individuals expressing their feelings intensely. Nor do blacks see sensibilities as so weak that they cannot withstand a forthright expression of opinion. Hence the comment "If someone has something to say about me, I want to hear it" from the black cultural standpoint is not especially brave, since blacks regularly confront each other in a direct manner as a matter of course. Moreover, they consider it cowardly and devious that information about themselves should come from anyone other than the source in any other way than direct and forthright. This is especially true when what someone has said has already been said to others and is slanderous. This is called "talking behind someone's back" or, as one black woman called it, "bitchin' behind the barn"; and it is a social offense. The response in such a case is to confront the one alleged to have committed the offense. We have seen an occurrence of this pattern in the encounter between Ms. Redmond and Ms. Jackson in chapter 6. Marjorie Goodwin shows in some detail the structure of this interactional pattern and how it functions for young black females as a way to deal with and prevent slanderous gossip (1980, p. 681). Finally, blacks do not share the white view that the black emotionally intense response to an offense is an overreaction; it is seen as simply the customary way blacks would react when their sensibilities have been offended and their feelings activated and aroused. As Harrison put it,

> blacks are not known . . . to ever be totally desensitized, defused, or repressed in their emotions when dealing with definable antagonisms. A black person would not pussyfoot with an insult from a white—or a black—if rendered with the slightest edge of an acerbity that might threaten one's security: the response would be fully acted out, regardless of the name of the game which deems it necessary to be *sensitive* to the other feller. [1972, p. 150]

Consequently blacks find distressing as well as prejudicial the fact that whites regard a black emotional reaction to an offense major but its provocation minor. One black woman fired from a Chicago bank gave as an example a situation in which the white employees with whom she had been working occasionally made racial slurs. For a while she let these pass, but when she was convinced that her fellow workers had also been tampering with her purse when she was away from her station, she reacted emotionally and vociferously. The white bank managers involved were barely concerned with the racial slurs and prejudicial acts that provoked her response. Rather, their behavior indicated that they believed the *real* problem to be the emotional intensity of her reaction, which to whites in that context suggested not merely lack of self-control but more general psychological instability.

Blacks, on the other hand, do not see emotional reactions to "definable antagonisms" as the problem, since responding to such feelings is for them simply being "for real." As Harrison put it, "It is behavior which gives affirmation to an inner essence which seeks when the organism is under duress, to achieve the necessary harmony required to be a complete man" (1972, p. 155). What is of greater concern to blacks, and what they regard as a more serious violation of the rights of others—but what whites consider hardly a violation at all—is to be in a situation where for compelling social reasons (such as keeping a job at a bank) they are not free to act in accordance with the force of their feelings. Blacks call this constraining mode of behavior fronting, and they generally regard negatively situations in which it is necessary to front. Whites do not typically notice when blacks front, since the mode—emotionally subdued—is one that whites consider normal, achieved as a matter of course in their cultural development through the habitual exercise of emotional self-restraint and repression. Consequently they are not aware of the conscious effort that blacks must make on a day-to-day basis to contain their emotions when working in what they regard as a racially hostile environment. All blacks consider fronting to be a strain. Some consider it downright painful, especially since black culture gives them the freedom to express their anger. This culture serves blacks in their effort to restore and maintain spiritual harmony, while white culture compels individuals to internalize and repress anger. Harrison considers fronting ("those anxious mental adjustments that are made in deference to the mode of oppression'') precisely the kind of social behavior that creates apparent conflicts in the black psyche. He considers those blacks who try desperately to hold the lid on and thus appear calm and collected by white standards the ones who should be watched. ''As Frantz Fanon observed, most black people play out the 'racial drama' down front because they have 'no time' to 'make it unconscious''' (Harrison 1972, p. 120, quoting Fanon 1967, p. 150).

Whites would consider this paradoxical, but blacks will regard a white context that allows them to express their feelings—even negative ones—as less alien than one in which they do not feel free to express feelings or act in accordance with their feelings at all. For whites an expression of negative feelings (such as anger) would signify that individuals have reached the stage where they are totally fed up with a situation, one in which their emotions can no longer be contained. Conversely, they would consider the absence of negative feelings a sign of contentment or at least acquiescence. Because of this difference, I regard nonassertion or nonexpression of feelings by black and white students quite differently. When blacks are behaving nonassertively or nonexpressively, I think that they have not as yet become comfortable enough to begin opening up. But I consider the same behavior by white students their basic cultural mode and thus not one that has any special significance.

The greater capacity of blacks to express themselves forcefully and to receive and manipulate the forceful assertions of others gives them greater leverage in interracial encounters at more intense levels of interaction. I have already remarked on this in chapter 2. It applies not only to classroom debate but to *argument* generally. One black woman remarked that she was always surprised at the difficulty her white college roommate had in contending with her when they had a difference of opinion. This observation has often been made by blacks, who consider whites as a result interpersonally weak as well as seeming to be ''forever demanding an apology over nothing.'' The basis for the last remark has already been established: whites consider an assault on the sensibilities of others a social offense. However, blacks do not consider the simple expression of opinions at a high degree of emotional intensity in the same way, especially since they regard the force of feelings as something that the sensibilities of others should be readily capable of withstanding.

But blacks also consider the demand of whites for an apology to be unjustified, because it suggests that the responsibility for the feelings and reactions of individuals belongs primarily to others, whereas blacks themselves consider individuals primarily responsible for their own feelings. Blacks will commonly say to those who have become angry, "*Others* did not make you angry"; rather, "You *let yourself* become angry." This parallels the view of blacks with respect to accusations, denials, and the assignment of guilt that was discussed in chapter 6. This view is that blacks stand accused only when individuals acknowledge the truth of the accusation by the way that they respond to it. "If the shoe fits, wear it" and "Only the truth hurts." But whites stand accused when *others* make an accusation: whites consider the social responsibility for protecting individual sensibilities—self-esteem—to belong primarily to others. Consequently, they can also call others to account when their sensibilities become offended. Blacks consider the responsibility for protecting individual sensibilities to fall primarily on individuals themselves. Perhaps for this reason, among others, blacks work hard to strengthen their individual capacity to withstand and manipulate the various forces with which individuals need to contend to maintain spiritual harmony—what blacks call "getting themselves together." Individuals develop and demonstrate their degree of togetherness by respectively developing and demonstrating their ability to contend. Black performers do so when they heat up the environment while, as Abrahams says, proclaiming their own cool (Abrahams 1976, p. 82). Black professional athletes do so when they execute extremely difficult feats without showing any visible strain (Greenfield 1975, p. 170). This cultural notion of togetherness is perhaps the central spiritual element within the larger conception of being *cool,* and constitutes a forceful ally for blacks in their continuing struggle to manage and manipulate the high-energy feelings within.

Feeling in Doing

Misunderstandings and conflicts also arise between blacks and whites because of their different views on the functional relevance of feelings in what Goffman has termed "guided doings," especially guided doings that are expressive (Goffman 1974, pp. 22–26). Blacks consider feelings here of fundamental importance, but whites consider them at best incidental, and at times even irrelevant. For example, a black and a white jazz musician on a Studs Terkel radio program in Chicago (aired July 17, 1979) were discussing the relative importance of technique and feeling with respect to both the historical development of jazz and playing jazz. The white musician considered only the importance of the development of technique. His black counterpart, however, said that he knew "lots of jazz musicians who got all the technique in the world but can't play worth a lick because they don't have the feeling." He added that that was why he could not play the blues. The white musician asked him incredulously, "You can't play the blues?" He answered, "Not really, because I'm too much concerned with technique. You got to have the *feeling* if you *really* want to play the blues."

The same difference in perspective was shown in a disco place. Allen Harris commented, on some music that was being played, "I can't dance to that." A white woman in the group said, "Oh, it's easy," and she proceeded to demonstrate the movements that corresponded to the dance being played. Therein she also demonstrated that for her, "knowing how" meant simply remedying a lack of information or technique, as the white jazz musician viewed playing the blues. But what Harris meant was that the music was not capable of activating the kind of feeling he needed in order to dance. Thereby he indicated that his expressive movements were directly responsive to his feelings. Notwithstanding his technical knowledge of the intricacies of the steps involved, without the right kind of music to activate the right kind of feeling, *he could not* dance.

In summary, the different consideration that blacks and whites give to feelings shows itself in many different situations. The one that occurs most frequently and is probably most troublesome socially for both blacks and whites comes about when activated black feelings threaten to override white established order and procedure. This situation has been discussed in chapter 2 with regard to turn-taking in the classroom when debate on an issue becomes heated. Here whites feel that blacks should be giving principal attention to white-imposed constraints against feelings becoming determinative. In just *coming in,* blacks ignore these constraints, following instead their own rules for entering into an ongoing presentation, giving greater consideration to the determinative and occasionally overriding force that activated feelings can have. When this happens, whites become indignant, viewing blacks as inconsiderate of the sensibilities of others who are showing proper emotional self-restraint in awaiting their authorized turn. They also view blacks as "socially immature" here, in not showing emotional self-restraint in awaiting their *own* proper turn.

Whites also become resentful, for example, when blacks, as audience members, respond verbally to some action that is taking place on the stage—following their call and response pattern—in a way that is out of place with respect to white structures and norms that have determined the proper intervals and kinds of audience response. Finally, whites are distressed when blacks let their feelings become too expressively intense, in disregard of established white norms and the sensitiveness of white sensibilities.

From their standpoint, blacks see whites as especially inconsiderate in not properly granting feelings the freedom to exert their own independent effect on proceedings. Blacks get upset when whites "hog the floor" in debate by not allowing them to come in with something immediately relevant. This prevents blacks from transferring the emotional energy of an impulse to the pulse of the proceedings, which they consider essential if the contentiousness of debate is to remain vigorous, animated, and individually involving. Nor do blacks like it when whites come down hard on them afterward because the expressive force of their feelings has overwhelmed individual sensibilities or violated white established norms. Blacks especially resent this last white reaction, because they regard structures inhospitable to feelings—like those of white culture—as constraining and artificial. Instead of being chastised for investing spiritual energy in white proceedings, blacks feel that they should be credited with having given what would otherwise be a lifeless process the kind of vitality it needs to generate and sustain human interest and involvement.

Nine
Style

Style is an attitude that individuals within a culture express through their choice of cultural form—blacks prefer cultural forms that do not restrict their expressive capacities—and the way they choose to express themselves within a given form. By these standards, black style is more self-conscious, more expressive, more expansive, more colorful, more intense, more assertive, more aggressive, and more focused on the individual than is the style of the larger society of which blacks are part.

Style pervades every aspect of life, from how one is born to how one is buried. Every way in which the style of one group differs from that of another group is not only noticeable and recognizable; it is a difference that can evoke admiration and imitation or hostility and conflict.

Blacks have evoked the admiration of the larger society in the performing arts: in music, dance, the theater, and on the playing fields, where they also "perform." Their everyday attire and ways of walking, standing, talking, greeting, and so forth produce more mixed reactions. The schoolroom and the work place are of central importance to the functioning of American society, and there we find the greatest problems. Those settings are touched on in chapter 10. The present chapter is limited to some of the different ways in which blacks and whites express style in casual, everyday contexts and on the playing field.

Body Language

The way a person stands, leans, or moves can communicate intent, as we have seen. During an argument between blacks, a change in position may well indicate a preparation for physical combat. Examples of this significance of movement were given in chapters 2 and 3. More basically, even the simplest use of the body expresses cultural style. There is a difference between the way blacks and whites walk. As Paul Harrison says, "Rather than simply walk, we *move:* the swaying swagger of the hips and the bouncing, bopping head-shoulder motion associated with *bopping* are derived from a strong rhythmic mode of walking" (1972, p. 73).

This "strong rhythmic mode of walking" has direct links to black dancing, which "is not so much the steps but what you do going from step to step. It's the rubato [rhythmic flexibility] of the black body" [Alvin Ailey, quoted in Saal 1980, p. 64]. On the dance floor, when the underlying rhythm is let loose, the movement can become an explosive and daring statement of individual style: "a testament, in form and substance, of our peoples' power sensibility." When young black men *bop* down the street, their gait communicates the same power idea—an image designed to "give notice of one's intentions to harmonize whatever is necessary for one's survival" (Harrison 1972, pp. 67, 73). In walking, as in all other matters, style is of the essence. Kenneth Johnson has written, "*Where* the young black male is going is not as important as *how* he gets there . . . . The means are more important than the end" (1971, p. 19).

Black greetings are also stylized to convey forceful expression or exhibition, whether the greeting is an embrace, "giving skin," the black-power handshake, or the more extended and elaborate hand, elbow, and hip movements called *dapping* (Cooke 1972, pp. 33–43).

Dress

Obviously the fundamental purpose of clothes is to cover the body. Beyond this, groups differ in their style of dress and their view of what constitutes appropriate wear on different types of occasion. Blacks regard clothing as a way to make the most powerful statement about themselves that they can. Harrison observes that "the attitude of a garment, in texture and color, is ritualistically assembled to create the most potent image that one's Nommo [life force] can conjure. The image—sharp, mean, bad—is designated to harmonize the threat of any force that might question one's humanity; its effectiveness is validated by the community's affirmative response" (1972, p. 32). On the street, the effectiveness of one's appearance is validated by the greater personal space accorded young men who are powerfully well dressed. Edith Folb reports that street-wise black teenagers in Los Angeles tend to adopt a "hands-off policy" toward those dudes who are *clean.* Even hardheads—"those who are into physical fireworks [violence] rather than costuming"—give them grudging admiration and respect. One teenager put it this way: "Dude dress nice, stay clean, brother maybe think twice 'fore he mess 'im up" (Folb 1980, p. 111).

The respect and admiration that blacks receive from their peers for the vital imagery of their costume often contrasts markedly with the reception they get from whites in official settings such as school. There whites tend to adopt a strictly utilitarian attitude toward clothing. Hats are outer wear, designed to protect the head from the cold as sunglasses are designed to shield the eyes from the sun. Once indoors, whites expect outer wear to be removed. But blacks consider hats and sunglasses *(shades)* artistic adornments, like jewelry, calculated to "effect a magical attitude," one that is neither motivated by nor responsive to white notions of pure utility (Harrison 1972, p. 33). When whites insist that once inside blacks remove their hats and sunglasses, the latter balk, for this would create an entirely different image from the one that they took great care to prepare that morning—a preparation that took into account the various places in which their costume would be worn. Much conflict between black students and white school officials occurs because of their different attitudes toward clothing.

"I'm on, Daddy, I'm on"

The black's method of combining movement and dress to activate powerful and expressive imagery is in itself a performance, even if the individual is about to do no more than walk down the block. The professional performer is especially aware of this situation. As Sammy Davis, Jr., said, "as soon as I go out the front door of my house in the morning, I'm on, Daddy, I'm on" (quoted in Messinger, Sampson, and Towne 1962, pp. 98–99). Often the stylized routines of the professional performer continue until, and sometimes include, the moment the performance itself begins.

J. P. ("Jellyroll") Morton has described the type of ritual that each jazz piano player back in the twenties went through before playing a note on the keyboard. As reported by Harrison, the ritual included

> the stroll from the café's doorway with a certain gait, through
> the audience and over to the piano, the tucking of the overcoat
> inside out to expose the red lining, the folding of the coat,
> placing it carefully on top of the piano, cane and hat on top of
> coat, and then, with calculated exaction, the suspending of the
> hands over the keyboard at the proper angle to allow the dia-
> mond rings to reflect the light and sparkle, just for a moment,
> before striking the keyboard to make one's *own* note. One's
> *own* signature completed the harmony of the ritual.
> [Harrison 1972, p. 33]

It is characteristic of black performers in general to view their entire time in front of the public as performance time. Muhammad Ali clearly does so, using whatever time he gets in front of the television cameras to display his verbal power—his boasting and bragging ("campaigning") or ring verse ("Feats of Clay")— which is all of a piece with his powerful performance in the ring, his boxing skill and showboating ("The Ali Shuffle"). Baseball player Reggie Jackson extends and accentuates the vitality of his individual image by managing to be alone on the field during the playing of the national anthem, which ritually occurs after the teams have had their warm-up practice and returned to the dugout. Jackson arranges this easily and inconspicuously: as Allen Harris has commented, he simply does not return to the dugout with his teammates after the warmup.

Individual Style

The group quality of black performance—call and response, coming in, dropping out, and interaction between the individual and the group—has been described in chapter 8 and elsewhere in this book. The individuality of the performer, the unique quality of his style, is also vital.

The performer's individual power is acknowledged by the audience's immediate and ongoing confirmation of the intensity of the image that is being created. This functions as the response but also as a further call to the performer to generate an even more powerful image. As Roger Abrahams has said (1976, p. 9), the performer's task "is not to make a thing but to bring about an experience in which not only his creative energies but the vitality of others may find expression." Thus the black performer's role is not just to demonstrate but also to instigate: to have the power of the created image function as an invocation (call) that serves, as Harrison puts it, "to galvanize the collective unconscious" from which the performer and the audience together draw spiritual sustenance (1972, p. 157).

Black performers, however, want the powerful images they generate to be indisputably their own. Often their nicknames reflect their success in achieving this status. Professional basketball player Lloyd Free got his nickname "World" from his playground teammates when they saw him turn 360° in the air one day and slam-dunk the ball on the way down (Elderkin 1979, p. 17). Walt Frazier got his nickname "Clyde" from the movie *Bonnie and Clyde*, not only because he wears flamboyant clothes but also because of his daring style of play, "stealing balls, gambling all the time and dribbling behind my back to escape pursuers" (Frazier and Berkow 1974, pp. 20–21).

The performer who tries unsuccessfully to perfect an individual style or is thought to be performing in someone else's style is regarded much less highly. Indeed, such people are usually treated with scorn or indifference. That is why black performers who are relative newcomers to the public scene tend to resent and resist comparisons with established black performers. When George McGinnis first came into the National Basketball Association from the rival American Basketball Association, he said, "People compare me with Connie Hawkins or Elgin Baylor but I think I have my own style" (in Lamb 1975, p. 36). And when a white television sports announcer interviewed a young black fighter after his bout and compared his fighting style with Muhammad Ali's, Greg Page protested, "There was only one Muhammad Ali. Let there be only one Greg Page."

Baseball player William Mays Aikins, named after the illustrious Willie Mays, has expressed displeasure over the constant reference and comparison to Mays, caused by the similarity of their names, which has made it more difficult for him to create his own public identity. His problem was reinforced when he joined his new team and his old number was not available. One of the few numbers available, and the one he finally chose, was the same number that Willie Mays had worn. He chose the number with some hesitation. "I don't want people to think I'm trying to copy Mays. I just want to be known for myself and my own accomplishments" (in Eldridge 1980, p. 18).

The emphasis on developing one's own style also helps to explain why one does not see in the black community the kind of public imitation of star performers that one finds in the white community, which welcomes "Beatlemania" and duplicate Elvis Presleys. No blacks with talent would be content simply to copy the style of other performers, no matter how famous, in lieu of developing a style of their own. To do so would signify to other blacks a lack of individual resourcefulness, imagination, and pride.

It would also be regarded as a presumption of another individual's ability, since blacks generally acknowledge performers, as artists, to be sole proprietors of the images they create through stylistic performance. To copy them would be an infringement of individual entitlement. For individuals to copy the performances of others and attempt to pass them off as their own would be an even worse violation. This is why blacks bristle at the very thought of white performers over the years getting the credit and reaping the benefits for simply reproducing styles that individual black performers originated and developed.

Of course blacks would be equally displeased to have their individual performance style or image co-opted by other blacks. All black performers want clear and undisputed entitlement to the image that they have personally developed and are publicly claiming for themselves. They do not always get it, however, since disputes occasionally arise among blacks over who has the greater right to a particular image, style, or title. One less than serious example of such a dispute was partially instigated and reported by sports reporter Don Pierson, in his effort to drum up additional interest in the 1979 Super Bowl confrontation between the Dallas Cowboys and the Pittsburgh Steelers. Pierson told Dallas linebacker "Hollywood" Henderson that the Steelers' lineman L. C. Greenwood had said Henderson had stolen Greenwood's nickname. This would also imply that Henderson had co-opted the "Hollywood" image that he had been publicly flaunting. Henderson's response was to defend his own greater entitlement to the "Hollywood" label, while discrediting Greenwood's: "L. C. Greenwood? L. C. Greenwood? I never heard anybody call him Hollywood. They must call him Hollywood in Pittsburgh in practice. They call me Hollywood everywhere" (Pierson 1976, sec. 6, p. 2).

Henderson's playful put-down of Greenwood ("They must call him Hollywood . . . in practice") indicates the "jive" nature of the dispute. On the other hand, for Greenwood's accusation to function even as a playful provocation indicates the seriousness with which blacks typically regard attempts to co-opt their individual public style (see chap. 3 for a fuller discussion of the relationship between "for real" and "play" verbal insults). This is not to imply that young black performers do not or should not incorporate stylistic features of established black performers in developing their own performance style. They do, in a time-honored tradition in the black community. But when they do, it is important to give proper credit to the source and then not to take on so much of another performer's style as to become a mere copy. Sugar Ray Leonard's fighting styles and skills—especially the quick hands—are clearly reminiscent of Sugar Ray Robinson. And there would have to be some stylistic similarity between the two for Leonard even to consider using the same nickname. But Leonard also has a distinctive style and has been quite open in acknowledging his indebtedness to the influence of Robinson and other established fighters. Blacks would regard Leonard's assumption of the nickname "Sugar Ray" not as an improper attempt to co-opt Robinson's fighting style and image but, rather, as a tribute.

Blacks are reluctant to imitate other black performers for another reason. It would be difficult to do so and avoid the implication that they were engaging in *marking* or signifying. For example, in marking (mocking), blacks affect the voice and mannerisms of other individuals in the context of narrating accounts of actual events in which such individuals played roles (in Mitchell-Kernan 1971, p. 137). Sometimes the characterization, or marking, of such individuals is neutral, for the purpose of making an account of an event more realistic or dramatic. More often the narrator marks others at their expense since, as Claudia Mitchell-Kernan has noted (1971, p. 139), the characterization of others is typically unflattering and as much a parody of the voice and mannerisms of the target as a pure imitation.

The usual context in which marking occurs is informal, typically in front of individuals with whom the marker is on familiar terms and who either share the same negative opinion of the marked person or can be counted upon to be amused rather than offended by the characterization. It is almost unnecessary to add that the targets are not present when they are being marked. However, occasions also arise when individuals are marked to their faces as a taunt, at which point blacks would also consider the marking to be signifying, unmitigated by an attempt to define it as play. A well-known example of marking used in this way can be found in the *toast*—a black folk tale in verse called "The Signifying Monkey," which Harrison considers "a household pet in every black community" (1972, p. 49; see also Abrahams 1964, pp. 136–41). Moreover, should the marking be done before a wider audience, it implies that the marker, in addition to signifying, is also trying to front off another person. We have already examined the provocative aspects of fronting someone off in chapter 7. One example of marking someone this way was reported to me by my colleague Ken Johnson. It occurred in a football game between the Pittsburgh Steelers and the Houston Oilers. Pittsburgh's L. C. Greenwood had just caused Oiler Billy ("White Shoes") Johnson to fumble. Greenwood picked up the loose ball and ran it into the Houston end zone for a Steeler touchdown. He then mimicked the "hully-gully" dance routine that "White Shoes" Johnson typically goes into after he scores a touchdown and that has become Johnson's personal signature. Greenwood's marking of Johnson to his face and before the capacity crowd constituted signifying as well as an attempt to front Johnson off, as if to say, "You ain't nothin'!"

Impersonations of famous blacks by performers in shows or on television would also count as marking them to their face and before others. Consequently, it would carry with it all the implications that blacks customarily associate with marking, signifying, or fronting someone off, put-downs or provocations rather than flattery. Thus it was probably significant that, in a televised benefit honoring Muhammad Ali, the only impersonation of Ali's voice and mannerisms came from white actor Billy Crystal. Since imitation can and does conventionally function as a sincere form of flattery for whites, Crystal's imitation of Ali's style in the context of praising him probably did not seem at all incongruous to Crystal.

Constraints on Performance Style

Black style, like other styles, is learned very early in life. The young black male bopping down the street, practicing the style he is still developing, tests his success—as both Folb (1980, p. 111) and Harrison (1972, pp. 32, 73) have noted—by whether his peers pay proper respect to his movement and his attire ("Dude dress nice . . . brother think twice").

Although black performers strive to develop their own style within the larger framework of black style, for their style to be accepted by their peers it must succeed, that is, be "together." An attempt to manifest style in performance without regard to the totality of the context, purpose, or nature of the event invites disapproval, even ridicule. Harrison (1972, p. 33) reports that a young, gifted black singing group from San Francisco repelled the audience at Harlem's Apollo theater despite the vigor of imagination they brought to their songs and choreography, because their costumes—net tank shirts, bell-bottomed levis, and sandals, the trappings of hippiedom—were inappropriate.

Performance Style in Sports

In others contexts the same standards for stylistic acceptance apply. For example, it would not be a matter for admiration how high a basketball player leaped, or how long he was able to suspend himself in mid-air, if on freeing himself for the shot he missed the basket. Ken Johnson gave me an example of a black card player who, at a critical point in the game, threw a card down from his hand with a great flourish, only to discover that it was the wrong card. This mental lapse immediately canceled whatever credit for style he might have gained from others had he thrown the right card down. As Johnson put it, "his manner of throwing the card down was nullified by his having thrown the wrong card down." Edwin McDowell cites a black Pittsburgh Steeler who, thinking he had reached the end zone, "spiked" the football ten yards short of the goal line. Another player, after catching a pass and thinking himself in the clear, stopped running and started prancing with the ball while he was still twenty yards short of the end zone, only to lose the ball when an opposing player hit him from behind (McDowell 1976, p. 16). Muhammad Ali introduced his famous "Ali Shuffle" in his first fight with Frazier, which he lost. When stylistic expression is not accompanied by a successful execution, the result is humiliating, because the audience regards a performer as having laid claim to greater expertise than he can demonstrate. As the saying in the black community goes, "everything must come together" (Holt 1972a, p. 60). To the extent that everything has not come together, black style cannot succeed.

Conflicting Styles on the Field and Court

Basketball players Julius Erving ("Doctor J") and John Havlicek epitomize black and white styles of playing basketball. Jeff Greenfield has contrasted the two:

> Erving has the capacity to make legends come true; leaping from the foul line and slam-dunking the ball on his way down; going up for a lay-up, pulling the ball to his body and throwing it under and up the other side of the rim, defying gravity and probability with moves and jumps. Havlicek . . . brings the ball downcourt, weaving left, then right, looking for a path. He swings the ball to a teammate, cuts behind a pick, takes the pass and releases the shot in a flicker of time. It looks plain, unvarnished. But there are not half a dozen players in the league who can see such possibilities for a free shot, then get that shot off as quickly and efficiently as Havlicek. . . .
> "White" ball then, is the basketball of patience and method. "Black" ball is the basketball of electric self-expression. [Greenfeld 1975, p. 248]

Greenfield's apt description of some of the differences between white and black ball playing makes it clear that one can expect to see conflict as well as conflicting styles on the field and court. This conflict has occurred, although it has lessened as white coaches learn to work with their black players and some white players who also "play black." The differences in style, however, are not so easily resolved, because they are based on differences in cultural attitudes—attitudes not only about expressiveness but also about competition, winning and losing, and even (perhaps especially) about the nature and definition of individuality within the context of team play.

The Team

The traditional white conception of a sports team is that of a group working together toward one goal—to win and, moreover, to accomplish their plays in the most efficient, economical, and cooperative manner possible. Underlying this concept is an assumption about the process of accommodation: the extent to which individuals are expected to adapt themselves to fit within the team's framework and the extent to which the team's management can or will adapt to the individuality of any given player. There are also accepted limitations on the extent to which individuals can shape or define their activity or role on the team.

John Havlicek, former basketball star of the Boston Celtics, alludes to all of this in attempting to account for the Celtics' losing streak during the 1977–78 season. He compared the team to that fielded by the Celtics during the period when they won eight straight championships: "We used to be a team of what I call role players.... That is, we were asked to concentrate on doing things well for the good of the team. We had people who were willing to sacrifice—who were willing to fit their talents and our style of play together in what would become a winning combination" (in Elderkin 1977b, p. 11). A team player, then, was a role player. Athletes, like executives, were confronted with organizational standards to which they were expected to conform. The plan for shaping a winning team had already been established by management. Maneuvers and patterns were set, requiring only proper execution. Certain positions called for certain attributes and skills: height, weight, strength ("muscle"), speed, agility, intelligence. Individuals were further typed to fill preconceived and idealized roles (e.g., "playmaker" or "rebounder"), all of them justified in terms of their utility. Although chosen for their "flexible" approach and attitude, individual athletes were rarely allowed flexibility in their approach to the game. Athletes were expected to "carry out their assignment to the best of their ability," without individual embellishment and, above all, without challenge to authority. As Havlicek's former coach Red Auerbach said, "When I coached, I was like a dictator. When I told my players something, I never wanted to hear the word 'why,' or anything like that. I just wanted a reaction" (in Elderkin 1977b, p. 11). Former basketball player Alex Groza compared playing under University of Kentucky Coach Adolph Rupp to being in the army: "He made the rules and we obeyed them.... There was no joking, no laughing, no singing, no whistling, no horseplay, no breaks in practice and certainly no questioning of his rules. He had us so wrapped up in basketball and winning that we didn't have time for anything else" (in Elderkin 1977a, p. 8).

Today some analysts regard the "martinet" manager as a

throwback to an earlier era, partly because players now have greater leverage with the front office and the fans. Baseball manager Gene Mauch says, "Today a disciplinary action means a quiet talk in the manager's room, with the door closed. The manager who chews a player out in front of the others is in deep trouble. It's a different world today" (in Rumill 1978, p. 16).

Yet white players are still obliged to subordinate those aspects of individuality that might interfere with the efficiency with which a team can be managed. Individuals who require excessive consideration ("coddling") and those who display temperament ("prima donnas") are still generally scorned, though they may be tolerated because of their ability. Unconventional lifestyles and habits (e.g., Bill Walton's vegetarianism) are deplored for the same reason. And of course the white management still retains sole authority and responsibility for defining the individual players' roles.

This is not to say that individuals have not achieved distinction or star status within this framework. But being singled out depends upon a combination of the individual's ability in an assigned role and the degree to which that role is instrumental in the team's success. Capable tall men are invariably singled out in basketball because their height and ability are crucial to the team's success. Good back court players are those who can bring the ball safely up to the front court, engineer the team's attack, and remain poised under pressure. Other individual qualities that enhance a team's chance of winning, such as hustle and aggressiveness, are valued and rewarded on the court and field. However, aspects of individuality that do not directly contribute to the team's efficiency are not considered relevant. And to the extent that the individuality of a player becomes a matter for consideration, whites would judge it a liability, detracting from both individual performance and effective team play.

Thus it was not an individual point of view but that of the majority culture that sportswriter Elderkin revealed in his interview of Havlicek. Elderkin indicated that he felt that the then slumping Celtics would only begin to recover their former preeminence when they decided to "return to the concept of a team with interchangeable parts" (in Elderkin 1977b, p. 11).

Expressive Play and Showboating

Into this highly structured and tightly managed team framework comes the black athlete and player, guided by cultural norms that not only sanction but promote, encourage, even demand that individuals "do their thing" or "showboat." As Holt puts it, it is "the only way one can present the person/self in a manner worthy of that self" (1972a, p. 60).

The black athlete, then, adds elements of performance style—vitality and individuality—to the team's shared goal of winning the game. Black players improvise, adding to the play some personal routine or maneuver that will make the play more dramatic and individually distinctive. Black players seek to go beyond the mechanics or technical aspects of play, intending to perform not simply proficiently but with flair. Blacks "prance and dance" for the sake of art and style as well as the sake of the game. White players might also be allowed to prance and dance on the playing field, but only for the sake of the game, as when they are working their way toward the end zone. Black players are more conscious of the powerful statement they are making when they execute such maneuvers on the field. They also show their independent concern with artful showmanship during official pauses within the game, as in the end zone after a touchdown has been scored, which McDowell has called the "Touchdown Follies,"

> that brief interim after a score when the ball carrier goes into anything from a leadfooted buck-and-wing to something that would pass muster on the stage of Radio City Music Hall.
>
> As football fans know by now, Touchdown Follies come in all shapes, sizes, and descriptions—not just the dances listed above but one-act plays culminating in melodramatically spiking the ball into the turf or letting it dribble down one's back in a tantalizing, controlled descent. [McDowell 1976, p. 16]

The Touchdown Follies occur after the points have been made. But more often than not, blacks also demonstrate their showmanship while making the point. In basketball, they do not simply lay the ball in for an uncontested basket. That would be too prosaic. Rather, with the ball in both hands, they leap as high as they can and slam it through the hoop (Greenfield 1975, p. 170). The height of the leap is functional, since it increases the players' chances of making the basket. At the same time, it is electrifying, and thereby gains credit for the player from his peers for having performed with style. As Greenfield says, "when you jump in the air, fake a shot, bring the ball back to your body, and throw up a shot, all without coming back down, you have proven your worth in uncontestable fashion" (1975, p. 170).

The dual goal is clear: not only to make the point but to project the most powerful image possible while making it. If either objective is not met, blacks will not regard the performance as successful. This is why they occasionally make the execution of a simple task more difficult, thereby turning its achievement into a more powerful statement. On the other hand, they often realize the same effect by making exceedingly difficult tasks look simple. Julius Erving does this when he appears to be making a simple, straightforward move in getting off the mark past his opponent, until one discovers that he has covered the distance from the foul line to the basket in one step, while more mortal players need to take two. Professional basketball player Darryl Dawkins carried the idea of power behind the slam-dunk to its logical limit when he shattered the backboard while slam-dunking the basketball in a few games during the 1979–80 season. He also carried to the limit the idea that such powerful slam-dunks are functional. He made the baskets and scored the points, so strictly speaking, they were functional, but at the expense of another phase of the game: the need to maintain continuity of play.

Showboating, as the word itself implies, is entertainment, and the use of showboating within the framework of a competitive event like basketball or football is an extension of the black cultural view that contests are a form of entertainment and that competition provides the atmosphere in which performers can best perform (see Abrahams 1970, p. 42). For blacks every game has a dual purpose: to win and dominate one's opponent, to be sure, but also to showboat, to demonstrate individual skill and style simultaneously. Depending on the score or the team standing, one element or the other is likely to surface. When one team is well ahead in the game and the outcome clearly decided, black players consider it show time. Harold Thomas, one of my students and a former basketball player, put it this way: "The showboating, or razzle-dazzle display, would begin only when the team was well ahead by twenty-five points or so, and rather than simply go ahead and win by sixty, we would start to showboat to entertain the crowd."

Within the framework of competition, black performers often use an opponent to highlight their own superior abilities and to showboat. In his prime, Muhammad Ali would demonstrate his dominance in the ring and then use his opponent to demonstrate his showmanship. The Harlem Globetrotters regularly use an opposing team as a foil to contrast their own showboating ability. The black pattern, then, is this: once the outcome of a game is clear, the adversary no longer needs to be vanquished. But the adversary can serve a further role, contributing to the crowd's entertainment. It may not make an opponent happier to find himself being used to help a superior player show off, but it does keep the crowd in the stadium. White players have no other option, once the outcome has been decided, than to make their behavior appear as though the outcome were still in doubt. The game becomes a charade—what white players call "going through the motions." And it is at this point that the crowd, with five minutes of game time still remaining, begins to file out.

Blacks also consider it permissible for players on the losing team to showboat. Once the outcome has been decided, individual members of the losing team can also do their thing. "Hollywood" Henderson was thus not at all reluctant to flash his "Hollywood" smile and his "number one" sign when the television camera zoomed in on him during a game, even though Dallas was losing. Unfortunately for Henderson, this act cost him his job with the Dallas team. White coaches might tolerate showboating when the team is winning, but not when it is losing. The reason the Cowboy management gave for Henderson's dismissal was "lack of concentration."

Conflict and Confluence

If an athletic team is to be run like an army, ideally consisting of "interchangeable parts," with players given no latitude to define their individual roles, what does the traditionally minded coach do with a player who insists on doing his own thing? If efficient accomplishment of a task is the goal and an athlete makes extra and seemingly unnecessary moves, doesn't this challenge authority and interfere with discipline? And how do white players, asked to subordinate *their* individuality to the team effort, look upon black players who use every opportunity to draw attention to themselves on the court by magnifying aspects of their performance that clearly serve ends other than scoring or winning? One might reasonably expect that the first reaction of such a coach would be to tighten the rules and that the first reaction of the white players would be to retaliate against the exhibitionistic black player to get him to curtail this kind of behavior. This has been the case.

Some white coaches have tried to solve what they see as problems created by black style by simply cracking down on the players. One such instance occurred at a midwestern university. The black football players responded by filing a list of grievances with the school administration against their white football coach, accusing him of racial discrimination. Among their grievances was the charge that the coach tried to keep them from showing emotion on the playing field. The specific instance cited occurred at the end of a practice session when blacks were doing a lot of congratulatory hand slapping. The coach called the team together and, according to the allegation, told the players to "keep those goddamn gestures at home" (Hersh and Berler 1980, p. 125).

In addition to cracking down, white coaches and sports officials added rules prohibiting certain kinds of behavior. The usual reason for adding or changing a rule is to keep one team from having an unfair advantage. In the 1942–43 season, George Mikan, a white player on the DePaul University basketball team, "batted a dozen Kentucky shots away from the basket by out-and-out goaltending. There was no rule against goaltending then, but it became illegal as soon as Kentucky's coach Adolph Rupp got the attention of the rule makers" (Enright 1980, p. 50). Mikan was much taller than any other player on any other team. Eliminating goaltending was necessary to give other teams a more equal opportunity against teams with very tall players.

But how can one explain the rule that penalizes spiking the football in the end zone during college games? The player who does this is not threatening to gain an advantage—play itself is officially in a state of pause. Showboating, the Touchdown Follies, cannot affect the conduct of the game or the score. Thus the rule that penalizes spiking the football could have been designed only to curb black expressiveness, to repress what whites see as immodest, unrestrained, and self-congratulatory gloating over one's own achievement. Professional football rules still allow spiking the football in the end zone after a touchdown has been made, but nowhere else. Consequently several black players have seen their entire run for a critical first down cancelled because, in their exuberance over their success, they spiked the football to punctuate their achievement.

Blacks are not, however, so limited that they cannot counter repression in one area with expression in another. As Ken Johnson told me, "if they outlaw spiking the football on scoring a touchdown, blacks will just dance more, and that's all right, because I'd rather see them dance. If they outlaw touchdown dances, blacks will come up with something else." Anthony Carter of the University of Michigan came up with "something else" equally thrilling after he scored one of his team's winning touchdowns in the 1981 Rose Bowl game. A friend of mine watching a telecast saw him "leap like a ballet dancer into the waiting arms of a black teammate, after which they hugged and danced around a little in front of the goal post."

Some white players felt particularly challenged by the behavior of black athletes who were joining their own and opposing teams. For one thing, white players resented the grandstanding and showboating of blacks, offending as it did then, and to a lesser extent still now, white norms of modesty and understatement (see chap. 4). Whites had certain rules against "hotdogging" it and playing to the crowd. Proper decorum for the baseball player who had just hit a home run, for example, was to acknowledge the crowd's applause simply by touching the tip of his cap while circling the bases. The same understatement applied to the player who had just made a spectacular catch. One who did any more would be seen as not simply responding to applause but cultivating it and would be negatively cast as a prima donna or as wanting too much of the limelight. A player was not supposed to enjoy his own accomplishment. Reggie Jackson receives criticism from some white baseball announcers for appearing to savor the home run he has just hit. Jackson stands at home plate and watches the ball go into the stands before he begins to circle the bases.

In contact sports like football and basketball, whites have regarded black showboating as crowing or gloating over the defeat of an adversary, which they consider poor sportsmanship. Thus, when one black football player had just scored a touchdown and was prancing about the end zone with the football raised in his hand—the Touchdown Follies were just getting started—a white player from the opposing team ran by and knocked the football out of his hand.

Bob Cousy, former Boston Celtics basketball superstar, displayed a similar reaction to black showboating near the end of a game in which the New York Knickerbockers had pulled well ahead of the Celtics. With the game in hand, "Sweetwater" Clifton of the Knickerbockers considered it show time and started to do some of his former Harlem Globetrotter tricks with the basketball. Cousy viewed Sweetwater's antics as an attempt to humiliate him and his teammates, notwithstanding the fact that Sweetwater was obviously playing to the crowd. Consequently, Cousy got even with Sweetwater by confronting him and embarrassing him with a slick basketball maneuver of his own.

The differences in the way blacks and whites approach basketball, football, and other competitive sports account for these confrontations. Whites view competitive sports exclusively in terms of winning and losing. Blacks view competing in sports in terms of dominating the field, being the best, and performing in a show. To whites, showboating within a game is directed only against one's opponent rather than, as blacks intend it, toward the crowd in the stands.

There are other reasons underlying the hostile reaction of whites to black style. One is that whites view many of the moves that blacks make for style to be irrelevant to the concepts of "team" and "winning." They are considered extraneous to the concept of efficiency, which requires that only simple, straightforward, and necessary moves be made. In terms of economy and winning, therefore, extra maneuvers can be regarded as at least wasteful and extravagant. At worst, individual style can be regarded as subversive, a threat to the white team concept, because an athlete who does his own thing implies that he is no longer properly subordinating himself to the complete authority of the coach.

This subordination, especially in the area of role definition, is the kind of accommodation that white coaches and players alike consider necessary to developing and maintaining a cohesive team and a concentrated effort. It is necessary to them because of the systems-oriented approach that traditional white coaches and managers use to define and govern individual and team play. They attempt to anticipate the various situations that might arise during the course of the game and to develop set plays in advance to cover each type of situation. This approach also leads players to produce lines of play for which set procedures have been established and to avoid lines of play that require individual initiative and improvisation. In setting up a tightly structured game plan beforehand, whites hope to increase their control over the course of the game. In doing so they sacrifice what they consider incidental and negotiable, but which blacks consider basic and non-negotiable, namely, spontaneity: being able to move and act as impulse, feelings, and intuition direct. Former New York high school star Bill Spivey said, "Cats from the street have their own rhythm when they play. It's not a matter of somebody setting you up and you shooting. You *feel* the shot. When a coach holds you back, you lose the feel and it isn't fun anymore" (in Greenfield 1975, p. 171).

Herschel Walker, the University of Georgia's freshman football star, says, "I watch game films of myself and Georgia's opponents because I guess all coaches like their players to study films. But I've never felt that I learned much from them. I think a good runner gets to where he's going by instinct or else he doesn't get there at all" (in Elderkin 1980a, p. 11). Connie Hawkins's criticism of the coaching style of former Los Angeles Laker coach Bill Sharman reflects the same attitude: "He's systematic to the point where it begins to be a little too much. It's such an action-reaction type of game that when you have to do everything the same way, I think you lose something" (in Greenfield 1975, p. 171). The valuable "something" that Hawkins thought was being lost was probably the vitality and individual creativity that develops when players retain the option to make improvised plays. Bill

Russell made a similar point in his autobiography: "Other things being equal, the artistic side of any sport will flourish whenever its players tend to dominate the game. The warlike side of a sport will flourish whenever the coaches and other nonplayers dominate" (in Russell and Branch 1979, p. 126).

I would also describe the coach-dominated white style of play as machine-like, characterized by mechanical repetition and interchangeable parts, although it is definitely also warlike in its exclusive focus on winning. Black emphasis on style and showmanship, on the artistic side of play and on individuality, constitutes both a threat and an antidote to this traditional white view.

The greater acceptance of black playing style today is in part a result of its commercial success. The fans not only want to see a winner; they also want to be entertained, and what and whom they pay to see has great influence with the front office. Coaches have become believers, too, because nothing succeeds like success, and blacks have demonstrated without question that their more individualistic style of play makes a team more effective.

This is partly because a team that uses only set plays often becomes too predictable. Set plays can succeed because of superior personnel or precise execution. But as teams become more closely matched and play each other often, predictability becomes more and more a liability. And it is here that the black style of play can make its special contribution, allowing individual players to go one-on-one—thus not only capitalizing upon the superior skills a player may have over the person guarding him but also taking advantage of blacks' culturally developed capacity for spontaneous improvisation, what Harrison (1972, p. 35) calls "mental reflex" and Albert Murray (1971, pp. 84–100) "riff-style" flexibility. Some early teams had considerable success in setting up individual black players to do their thing. The Buffalo Bills did, for example, when they organized their game around the running ability of O. J. Simpson. They not only highlighted his exceptional talents but also utilized them more fully than had been done before. Conversely, teams that are too systems-oriented often fail to utilize to the team's best advantage the exceptional gifts of individual players. This happened when Julius

Erving first joined the Philadelphia 76ers. Sportswriter Bill Fox reported that

> in trying to fit in with the flow, Erving has instead become a prisoner of its drift, allowing himself to abandon the improvisation which was his stock in trade.
>
> "The 76ers haven't built their team around Doc," says his former coach with the Nets, Kevin Loughery. "I know Doc. I know he's a winner. I see him play today though, and it amazes me. It just isn't the same Doc. Knowledgeable people keep telling me that now he is just another player." [Fox 1977, p. 10]

On the other hand, teams with too many star performers can suffer because each star wants the other players to cooperate in utilizing and magnifying his special talents. The Philadelphia 76ers were especially known for this problem at one time, and it is one that black players themselves recognize. Allen Harris recalled a situation when television sportscaster Keith Jackson had the three former Heisman trophy winners from the University of Southern California in his broadcast booth in 1976, during the final USC game against UCLA: Mike Garrett, Anthony Davis, and O. J. Simpson, all great running backs. He asked the television audience, "How would you like to be the coach of a team that had all three of these men in your backfield?" Simpson responded, "Which one of us is going to do the blocking?"

There is clearly a possibility for blending the best of white and black playing styles into a winning combination. The whites' need for players to accept certain roles for the good of the team and the blacks' need for the team to organize itself around the special talents of individual players can, when combined, produce both greater individual satisfaction and team success. The Chicago Bears are certainly no worse a team when they throw the football to Walter Payton out in the flat and help him demonstrate his brilliant broken-field running ability. Nor are the Philadelphia 76ers any worse a team when the other players clear the lane to allow Julius Erving to go one-on-one against his opponent. As Lloyd Free says, "I'm as much a team player as anybody, but let me tell you something. There are times when every team needs a great one-on-one player that it can give the ball to in a clutch situation who will get them the basket" (in Elderkin 1980b, p. 16).

When George McGinnis first joined the Philadelphia 76ers in 1975, there were already indications of some kind of confluence and perhaps accommodation between white and black styles of play. Gregory Lamb, who wrote the interview, first described McGinnis's special flair:

> When George makes a move to the basket, gliding through the air with fingers wrapped around the ball as if it were a grapefruit, he can make even the sophisticated fans of the NBA roar in astonishment.
>
> "I like to make an exciting move," he tells you, "but I'm not trying to showboat. I just like to have fun when I play—it's a means of expression for me . . . ."
>
> George seems to be happy with the role the 76ers Coach Gene Shue has given him on the team. "He has a lot of plays that use my individual talent and a lot of plays for the team," explains McGinnis. "We play together but everybody does his thing. It's a good system." [Lamb 1975, p. 36]

As coach, Shue seems to have given McGinnis some latitude to demonstrate his individual ability. McGinnis's statement that he was "not trying to showboat"—if we can believe that an "exciting move" isn't showboating—suggests that he too was being somewhat accommodating. Perhaps, in return for Shue's having "a lot of plays that use my individual talent" and shaping a team in which "We play together but everybody does his own thing," McGinnis cut down a bit on some of the more spectacular and improvisational aspects of his showboating style in order not to be viewed as setting himself too far above the rest of the team, something that is much more likely to offend whites than blacks.

There does not indeed appear to be any reason why individual skill and style cannot be incorporated at the planning stage into a winning team strategy on the court and field, as it has in dance, theater, instrumental groups, and even, as we saw earlier in this chapter, on the street. For the black performer, skill and style—the integral components of doing your own thing—are symbiotic. They draw upon and reinforce each other and combine to enable performers to make the most powerful statement of which they are capable. To encourage stylistic expression within a team effort, to plan and build around it, is thus to bring out the best in the individual black player and performer.

Ten

Epilogue

The examination of black and white conflict arising from differences in style needs to be carried further than has been done here, especially in the contexts of the schoolroom and work place. There the consequences of different cultural patterns, perspectives, and values affect not only the quality of black and white social interaction but (perhaps even more critically from the black standpoint) black social and economic success. These are, after all, contexts in which white standards alone usually determine what constitutes good performance and, consequently, where accommodation to black performance styles has been absent or at best negligible. They are also the contexts in which the white rule of "shape up or ship out" is most strictly followed.

Susan Houston has provided one example to point up this need.

In a school in southern Florida, Houston conducted an experiment in communication. She asked poor and well-to-do black and white first-graders—four groups in all—to remember every detail of a story so that they could repeat it exactly to a partner assigned to them. Analyzing the results, Houston found that there were marked differences in the way the poor black children carried out the assignment. One difference was the way they interpreted the instructions. The two white groups and the well-to-do black group took them literally. Consequently the versions of the story they told tended to match the original, both in length and accuracy of detail. The poor black children, however, used the instructions as a departure point from which to demonstrate individual imagination and creativity—Houston called it flair—reproducing general material from the original story but supplying their own details. As a result, 26 percent of the stories told by this group included original material, as against 12 percent or less for the other groups.

There were other differences, too. The poor black children interacted with other children far more often than did the other groups. For example, when they told the stories they attended principally to their partners, whereas the other children told their stories more with an eye on Houston, looking for her approval. The poor black group also made greater use of nonverbal behavior. Their gestures involved the whole body, in contrast to the more "confined" gestures of the white children (Houston 1973, p. 48).

The performance of the white and the well-to-do black first-graders reflected the cultural norms of the dominant society. Those children were *literal:* that is, they reproduced details correctly and repeated memorized material verbatim; they were *obedient:* they did not deviate from the instructions given by the adult in charge; and they were *modest:* they confined their gestures, thereby not calling special attention to themselves. Furthermore, there was little to distinguish one child's performance from that of another. This accords with another basic feature of white performance as a group: *uniformity* (see chap. 2).

In short, while these children were performing literally and uniformly, showing "proper" subordination of individuality to the demands of the task, the poor black children were literally performing, emphasizing both individuality and vitality, which, because of their cultural background, blacks have come to regard as essential to successful performance. This is especially true of performances within such a familiar and traditional black folk genre as oral narrative. As Paul Carter Harrison says, "style does not suggest any fixed limits on how a narrative or song must be delivered.... The alert songster or story teller exploits the context to achieve not only immediacy but also some variation on old themes.... The oral tale lives in the telling [and] draws its vitality from the context it is told in." Moreover, "the improvisational style of black speech precludes fixity of narrative or song styles"; change—"that aspect of order that revitalizes an event"—is more consistent with the traditional sensibility (1972, p. 7). By way of contrast, Walter Ong writes of being pulled up some years ago by a five-year-old—I presume white—when telling the story of The Three Little Pigs. He said, "He huffed and he puffed, and he huffed and he puffed," instead of the literal reading, "He huffed and he puffed, and he puffed and he huffed." Fixity of oral narrative within the white cultural group is the norm, and as Ong says, the young audience "expects the story as a whole and its formulary elements to be the same each time it is told" (1969, p. 640).

The different ways in which the poor black and the other children responded to the assignment, then, was consistent with their different cultural experiences. Furthermore, given the nature and purpose of the task, all of the children might reasonably have expected that their particular style of performance would be acceptable in a test situation. But this would not be the case. As Houston notes, had the experiment been a test, the poor black first-graders would have failed, notwithstanding their greater verbal creativity and more dynamic oral presentation (1973, p. 48). This is because, according to teachers and psychologists, a "good" performance is one in which students reproduce details correctly, avoid deviating from the norms set by the adult in charge, and repeat memorized material verbatim. The performance of the poor black children did not satisfy any of these criteria. It is also relatively easy to predict, therefore, that these poor black children will do worse in school—unless, of course, they repress their variant behavior and adopt the type of performance favored by whites.

But this raises other questions that relate to the practicability of such an exchange and, even more important, to its desirability in terms of the needs or goals of the individual and the larger society. Albert Murray notes that even when blacks set out to effect literal imitations of white people, they often seem to "find it impossible not to add their own dimensions" (1971, p. 84). Jack Daniel and Geneva Smitherman see black call and response as such a "natural, habitual dynamic in Black communication that Blacks do it quite unconsciously when rapping to other Blacks" (1976, pp. 37–38). Thus, even were these poor black children to cooperate with whites in repressing their own patterns of performance, they would find not only the process difficult but, most probably, their performance in the new style only marginally successful.

How desirable, in any case, is such a change? From the individual's standpoint there is the issue of identity and self-esteem. There is also the question of effectiveness. For example, even an adept and talented basketball player like Julius Erving found that his effectiveness diminished when he tried to suppress his flamboyant style of play to become a more "straightlaced" player (Fox 1977, p. 10). Only when he switched back to his more natural style did Erving regain his former stature as a superstar performer. Over the years, I have come across many black people who are fluent and confident speakers in their original dialect and style but who become hesitant and uncertain when they attempt to use the pronunciation, grammar, and style of white speakers.

The crucial problem is what the individual gains and loses by this exchange. The same question might be posed for the larger society: How much uniformity is necessary or desirable, and how much variation is valuable? George Castile (1975, p. 38) argues, for example, that the "evolutionary potential" of a society—(a principle taken from Marshall Sahlins and Elman Service [1960]) is better served by maintaining, rather than eliminating, cultural variation. Castile sees a danger in cultural systems overadapting and becoming overspecialized in order to accommodate specific circumstances that will limit or prohibit their flexibility of response to changing circumstances:

> Stable plural societies contain within themselves greater pools of variation from which responses to selective pressures can arise . . . Navaho views of the harmonious balance necessary with nature seem singularly useful in a society confronted with the outer limits of a world view based upon unlimited expansion and unlimited good. But it is not with specifics that we are concerned here but simply the value of variation itself. [1975, p. 39]

One might well consider the value to the larger society of black improvisational style: the ability to move through changes, what Harrison (1972, pp. 35–37) calls "mental reflex," as opposed to the white cultural mode of "mental set" that inhibits whites' flexibility to respond or adapt to changing circumstances. One might also consider the singular contribution of blacks to society in their concentration on performance. One white graduate student in theater in my department, who was also teaching English in one of Chicago's all-black high schools, rewrote the high school drama curriculum and changed it from a purely literary exercise—reading plays and discussing them—to include theatrical performance. In this way he not only revised the curriculum to take advantage of the performance of blacks, thereby making the plays as a whole more attractive to them; he enriched the curriculum for all students by introducing a way to achieve a deeper understanding of the plays than could be gained through reading and discussion alone (Bates 1977).

A colleague of mine, Frederick Erickson, provides an example from the work place that also points to the need to reconsider the present nonaccommodation of black performance style. A white foreman asked a group of black and white workers to move a number of fifty-pound boxes of cut steel from a platform and stack them on a wooden platform approximately one step and a 110° turn away from the table. The white workers accelerated quickly, throwing themselves immediately into the task, lifting the boxes from the table with short, jerking motions and setting them down again in the same fashion. The black workers moved more slowly into the task. But once into it, they used the weight

of their entire bodies to convert the entire job of lifting and placing the boxes into a single, fluid, continuous movement. The
movement here is similar to that used by some black running
backs in football. As Herschel Walker described his style,

> once the quarterback hands me the ball, I'm not what you'd
> really call a fast starter.... I never hit the line that quickly,
> because first you have to make sure you have control of the
> football. Fast isn't necessarily good if it cuts down on the time
> you need to see where you're going. I kind of pick my way
> through the secondary before I start to take advantage of my
> speed.... It's not anything anyone ever told me to do. It's just
> me. [In Elderkin 1980a, p. 11]

Erickson likened the movement of the black workers above to a
"slow-moving ballet." His view of their performance was not
shared by the white foreman, however, who was openly critical of
the blacks for not "hustling" and for not working as "hard" as
the white workers. Yet when the job was finished—all were
working on a piece-cost basis—the blacks had moved the same
number of boxes as the whites. Thus the foreman was reacting to
appearances—white images of what constitutes "hustling" and
"hard" work. The black rhythmic mode seemed to expend less
effort, which would make it, from his standpoint, as much play as
work.

In fact, as Erickson told me, the blacks' performance was
achieved with less strain because, in using the entire weight of
their bodies to move the boxes, they were more "energy-
efficient." And it is interesting to note that, at least in one midwestern steel plant, this method of moving cartons of cut steel has
become standard for all workers. As steel executive Nathan
Grossner told me, "I have watched workers in our plant move
cartons of steel. Some of them are white, but most are blacks,
Koreans, and Mexicans. They all move in the same fluid style
because that seems to be the way to do the job."

In sum, the presumption that the performance of a task is invariably better when white performance style is used needs to be
examined carefully. The presumption is certainly vulnerable
when it is made without comparative knowledge of the mode it is
attempting to displace or consideration of the disabling effect of
the substitution of another cultural mode for a habitual one.

This focus on cultural differences as a source of black and white conflict should not draw attention away from the potent effect of racial and social differences in black and white communication. Clearly, when a white high-school girl's response to a black male student's verbal rap is not annoyance but fear, racial and perhaps class difference account for the quality and intensity of her response—not merely a violation of white cultural norms as to how a woman should be properly met (see chap. 5).

Moreover, race must be seen as relevant even when class is not. Thus, a black reviewer of this manuscript noted that in her experience at academic meetings, whites withdraw from participation when blacks violate behavioral norms, but not when other whites do so (see chaps. 2 and 3). Indeed many studies show that the punishment meted out to blacks when they violate social and cultural norms is greater than that accorded to whites for the same offense. This differential treatment is clearly a matter of racial discrimination, and it should be emphasized that the same difference in treatment occurs at all social levels, even when what is involved is no more than a breach of decorum. Yet there are further grounds for blacks to feel indignant on this score, since whites often censure them for violating white norms even when blacks are behaving in ways appropriate to black norms. That no consideration should be granted blacks when they behave in accordance with their cultural norms, when this violates white norms, reinforces a pattern of black cultural subordination. Thus the greater severity of punishment of blacks when only white cultural norms are being violated is a double injustice. Blacks are judged not only in terms of white norms, instead of black ones, but more severely than are whites themselves.

The issue of cultural subordination has always been a powerful one for blacks. In recent times it has become more boldly disputed, and this will undoubtedly continue, as blacks work to achieve social parity for their own linguistic and cultural patterns. As many of the examples in this book show, much of the conflict that arises in school and at work is due to white attempts to proscribe black patterns on the basis of the notion that in mainstream contexts, at the very least, only standard (white) cultural patterns should be used. I have already noted the protest that black university students filed against their white football coach for engaging in racial (and cultural) discrimination. In another instance, white administrators in the recently desegregated Louisville school system issued a ruling forbidding students to wear hats inside school buildings. Black students, at whom the rule was particularly aimed, complied: they did not wear their hats inside the school buildings. Instead, they began to *carry* them ostentatiously. Their response was consistent with Ken Johnson's prediction that arbitrary white repression of black style in one area will simply be countered with black stylistic expression in another: "If they outlaw spiking the football on scoring a touchdown, blacks will just dance more . . . . If they outlaw touchdown dances, blacks will come up with something else."

Blacks and whites are caught up in a power struggle in which the social acceptability of black language and cultural patterns remains the central issue. Cultural differences are often treated simply as an irritant, not otherwise receiving the attention they deserve in themselves. As long as the struggle over social parity for the cultural patterns of blacks (and other minority groups) is unresolved, in all likelihood this will continue to be the case.

Appendix
Testing for Cultural Homogeneity

The terms *black* and *white* have been used in this book to designate, respectively, the cultural patterns and perspectives of black "community" people and the white middle class, principally because the material I have drawn on came from these two groups. However, my observations over the years of blacks and whites of different social levels lead me to believe that the patterns and perspectives described herein are not confined to these specific groups (see also Abrahams 1976, p. x). The extent to which they are shared by other groups has not been clearly defined; nor, for that matter, has the extent to which they are shared by black community people and members of the white middle-class other than those from whom the contrasting cultural information herein was obtained.

The lack of clear definition of the distribution of these cultural patterns is due in turn to the absence of any clear definition of the patterns themselves. It is difficult to find something when you are not quite sure what you are looking for. However, as I said in the introduction, I believe that the material in this book does provide a sufficiently clear delineation of black and white cultural patterns to enable investigators to begin to examine their distribution within different groups, not the least of which are the black and white populations themselves. I have started to do so in a preliminary way with the help of students; my approach and results are discussed below.

Two graduate students, Beth Caldwell and Allen Harris, conducted a survey of forty-nine blacks (twenty men and twenty-nine women) and forty-nine whites (twenty-seven men and twenty-two women) from the college population on my campus. The survey questionnaire, which Caldwell and I developed, dealt with material discussed in chapter 8 above. Specifically, the survey was designed to reveal differences in attitude or behavior that would be likely to result from the different priorities assigned to feelings and sensibilities within black and white culture.

The first two items on the survey were statements which asked for "true/false" responses:

1. It bothers me to criticize others.
2. It bothers me when others criticize me.

Item 1 was chosen to elicit the relative degree of concern that whites and blacks would express about offending the sensibilities of others. We expected that white students—especially females—would be "bothered" considerably more than black students, because whites regard individuals as more sensitive than do blacks. In criticizing others, whites run the risk of violating the injunction "If you can't say anything nice, don't say anything at all," thereby subjecting the violator to guilt feelings and possible recriminations for committing a social offense. We also expected white students to be more bothered by the criticism of others. Our hypothesis was that whites, who are more protective of each other's sensibilities, would therefore be more vulnerable and thus more easily offended by criticism than blacks. Not every respondent answered every question, but the results we received are in the table.

	Black men	Black women	White men	White women
1. It bothers me to criticize others.				
True	6	9	12	15
False	12	19	15	7
2. It bothers me when others criticize me.				
True	2	14	17	17
False	18	15	10	5

Two other items were listed. The first hypothetical situation was general; the second, more specific.

3. If someone were to do something that bothered me, I would
   a. hold back on my feelings for fear of hurting that person.
   b. tell the person how I felt.
   c. forget it.
4. If a member of the opposite sex were to approach me in a disco or lounge or singles' bar and I wanted that person to leave me alone, I would
   a. be stuck with that person because I would not be able to tell him or her I was not interested.

b. make an excuse by telling him or her that I was with someone else.

c. tell him or her that I wasn't interested.

Item 3 was intended to show whether blacks and whites would react differently in situations where their own sensibilities had been offended. Again we expected white students, especially females, to select responses that were less forthright—*a* or *c*—because of their training to remain polite in order to avoid offending someone else. We expected this even though the norms of white society give its members the right to assert themselves when they feel offended. Conversely, we expected black respondents to choose more forthright reactions, because responding to one's own feelings is of paramount importance within black culture, especially when blacks' own sensibilities have been offended.

Item 4 was chosen to test how blacks and whites would respond to a specific situation in which they had to choose between their own feelings—and perhaps also their own sensibilities—and the feelings and sensibilities of others. Yet again we expected white students, especially females, to choose the more inhibited responses, consistent in revealing an unwillingness or inability to act in accordance with their own feelings, in order to avoid offending others, even when they would become involved in an undesirable social situation. We expected them either to "be stuck" or to choose the less forthright method of escape—"make an excuse." We expected blacks, on the other hand, to be much more forthright, for two reasons: (1) black culture places more importance on feelings than on sensibilities—and therefore one's own feelings count more than someone else's sensibilities; (2) in the black view, other people are not so sensitive as to be overwhelmed by a straightforward reply. We also expected more forthright responses from blacks because of the special conventions governing black male and female interaction (see chap. 5). Black women are expected to be sexually assertive and forthright when black males express sexual interest in them. The results are in the table.

	Black men	Black women	White men	White women
3. If someone were to do something that bothered me, I would				
a. hold back	1	6	5	7

	Black men	Black women	White men	White women
b. tell	16	18	15	12
c. forget it	3	3	5	3

4. If a member of the opposite sex were to approach me in a disco or lounge or singles' bar and I wanted that person to leave me alone, I would

	Black men	Black women	White men	White women
a. be stuck	2	2	5	9
b. make an excuse	4	7	14	5
c. tell	11	18	6	6

The distribution of the responses met our expectations in general, although white men and white women favored more direct responses to Item 3 than we thought they might, as did white women to Item 4. In attempting to account for the responses of the white females, Harris and I noted that seven of the twelve most forthright responses to Item 3 and four of the six most forthright responses to Item 4 came from theater majors, whom both Harris and I consider more assertive than the average white female. On the other hand, several white males and females who chose the most forthright response to Item 3 indicated, by their response to Item 2, that they are sensitive to criticism from others. These individuals—especially the males—may represent a "high offense–low defense" group within the white population that I often see in my classes. Although such whites often act assertively when criticizing others, their own self-esteem remains vulnerable to assault. This often gets them into difficulty with blacks, for whom the ability to offer offense also implies the ability to defend oneself ("Don't say no more with your mouth than your back can stand"). Blacks generally, especially the males, responded to the questions like members of a "high offense–high defense" group. Their response supports my own views about black cultural development in general and, more specifically, the cultural development of black males discussed in chapter 3 above.

No statistical significance for the pattern of distribution of the responses is being claimed. For one thing, the respondents were all college students. The inclusion of the survey, therefore, is intended to serve a heuristic function both with regard to indicating possible trends within larger samples of black and white populations and to illustrate how the hypotheses about black and white cultural differences offered throughout this book can be used to test for cultural homogeneity within black and white racial populations—and perhaps cultural diffusion as well.

These hypotheses can also be used to determine what kinds of social, linguistic, and cultural criteria tend to correspond; hence they can offer insight into what kinds of linguistic and cultural acquisition and loss accompany the movement of blacks into the social mainstream (see Harris 1981). I would expect even sharper contrasts between middle-class whites, the *white* group I have been writing about, and blacks whose social network exists almost entirely within the black community and whose patterns and perspectives would be therefore more completely determined by the cultural values I have called *black*.

References

Aarons, Alfred A.; Gordon, Barbara Y.; and Stewart, William A., eds. 1969. *Linguistic-Cultural Differences and American Education. Florida FL Reporter* 7(1).

Abrahams, Roger D. 1964. *Deep Down in the Jungle*. Hatboro: Folklore Associates.

———. 1970. *Positively Black*. Englewood Cliffs, N.J.: Prentice-Hall.

———. 1972a. "Joking: The Training of the Man of Words in Talking Broad." In *Rappin' and Stylin' Out*, edited by Thomas Kochman. Urbana: University of Illinois Press.

———. 1972b. "The Training of the Man of Words in Talking Sweet." *Language in Society* 1(1): 15–29.

———. 1976. *Talking Black*. Rowley, Mass.: Newbury.

Ali, Muhammad, with Richard Durham. 1975. *The Greatest: My Own Story*. New York: Random House.

Animal Tales Told in the Gullah Dialect. 1949. Told by Albert H. Stoddard. Vol. 1. Sound Recording L 44. Washington, D.C.: Archive of Folk Song of the Library of Congress.

Atkin, Ross. 1979. " 'Hollywood Henderson' at Super Bowl." *Christian Science Monitor*, 18 January 1979, p. 16.

Baratz, Joan and Stephen. 1972. "Black Culture on Black Terms: A Rejection of the Social Pathology Model." In *Rappin' and Stylin' Out*, edited by Thomas Kochman. Urbana: University of Illinois Press.

Bates, Randall E. 1977. "The Justification and Construction of a Performance-based Drama Curriculum for the High School." M.A. thesis. Chicago: University of Illinois at Chicago Circle, Department of Communication and Theatre.

Bateson, Gregory. 1972. *Steps to an Ecology of Mind*. New York: Harper & Row, Chandler.

Bauman, Richard, and Sherzer, Joel, eds. 1974. *Explorations in the Ethnography of Speaking*. London: Cambridge University Press.

Beowulf. 1963. Translated by Burton Raffel. New York: Mentor.

Brown, H. Rap. 1969. *Die Nigger Die*. New York: Dial.

Castile, George P. 1975. "An Unethical Ethic: Self-Determination and the Anthropological Conscience." *Human Organization* 34(1): 35–40.

Cazden, Courtney B.; John, Vera P.; and Hymes, Dell, eds. 1972. *Functions of Language in the Classroom.* New York: Teachers College Press.

Charters, Samuel. 1963. *The Poetry of the Blues.* New York: Oak.

Collins, Leslie. 1968. "Rap, Baby, Rap." Xeroxed. Chicago: Northeastern Illinois University, Center for Inner City Studies.

Cooke, Benjamin G. 1972. "Non-verbal Communication among Afro-Americans: An Initial Classification." In *Rappin' and Stylin' Out,* edited by Thomas Kochman. Urbana: University of Illinois Press.

Daniel, Jack L., and Smitherman, Geneva. 1976. "How I Got Over: Communication Dynamics in the Black Community." *Quarterly Journal of Speech* 62:26–39.

Day, Beth. 1974. *Sexual Life between Blacks and Whites.* London: Collins.

Elderkin, Phil. 1977a. "Rupp: A Basketball Baron in the Land of Colonels." *Christian Science Monitor,* 23 December 1977, p. 8.

———. 1977b. "Those Sinking Celtics Just Out of Sync." *Christian Science Monitor,* 22 December 1977, p. 11.

———. 1979. "The Serious Side of a Supershowman." *Christian Science Monitor,* 4 April 1979, p. 17.

———. 1980a. "For Walker the Runner, Instinct Plays a Big Role." *Christian Science Monitor,* 16 December 1980, p. 11.

———. 1980b. "Showman of the Cagers." *Christian Science Monitor,* 26 December 1980, p. 16.

Eldridge, Larry. 1980. "Aikins, Bearer of a Famous Baseball Name, No Longer Lives in its Shadow." *Christian Science Monitor,* 17 October 1980, p. 18.

Enright, James. 1980. *Ray Meyer: America's #1 Basketball Coach.* Chicago: Follett.

Erikson, Eric H. 1968. *Identity: Youth and Crisis.* New York: Norton.

Fanon, Frantz. 1967. *Black Skin, White Masks.* New York: Grove.

Fisher, Lawrence E. 1976. "Dropping Remarks and the Barbadian Audience." *American Ethnologist* 3(2): 227–42.

Folb, Edith A. 1980. *Runnin' Down Some Lines: The Language and Culture of Black Teenagers.* Cambridge: Harvard University Press.

Fox, Bill. 1977. "Dynamite Duo Fails to Detonate." *Christian Science Monitor,* 21 January 1977, p. 10.

Frake, Charles. 1964. "A Structural Description of Subanum 'Religious' Behavior." In *Explorations in Cultural Anthropology,* edited by Ward

Goodenough. New York: McGraw-Hill.

Frazier, Walt, and Berkow, Ira. 1974. *Rockin' Steady*. New York: Warner.

Fuller, Edmund. 1978. "Of Beowulf, Boxing and the Ali Myth." *Wall Street Journal*, 28 February 1978, p. 18.

Garn, Stanley M. and Clark, Diane C. 1976. "Problems in the Nutritional Assessment of Black Individuals." *American Journal of Public Health* 66(1): 262–67.

Glazer, Nathan, and Moynihan, Daniel P. 1963. *Beyond the Melting Pot*. Cambridge: M.I.T. Press.

Goffman, Erving. 1967. *Interaction Ritual*. New York: Doubleday, Anchor.

———. 1974. *Frame Analysis*. New York: Harper & Row.

Goodwin, Marjorie H. 1980. "He-Said-She-Said: Formal Cultural Procedures for the Construction of a Gossip Dispute Activity." *American Ethnologist* 7(4): 674–94.

Greenfield, Jeff. 1975. "The Black and White Truth about Basketball." *Esquire* (October), p. 170.

Gregg, Richard B.; McCormack, A. Jackson; and Pederson, Douglas J. 1972. "The Rhetoric of Black Power: A Street-level Interpretation." In *Language, Communication and Rhetoric in Black America*, edited by Arthur L. Smith. New York: Harper & Row.

Gregory, Dick, with Robert Lipsyte. 1964. *Nigger*. New York: Pocket.

Haiman, Franklin S. 1972. "The Fighting Words Doctrine: From Chaplinsky to Brown." *Iowa Journal of Speech* 3(1): 3–31.

Harris, Allen. 1981. "Methodology for Determining the Effects of Acculturation on Mainstream American Blacks." M.A. thesis. Chicago: University of Illinois at Chicago Circle, Department of Communication and Theatre.

Harrison, Paul C. 1972. *The Drama of Nommo*. New York: Grove.

Hernton, Calvin C. 1966. *Sex and Racism in America*. New York: Grove.

Hersh, Phil and Berler Ron. 1980. "Racial Charges Irk Northwestern's Venturi." *Chicago Sun-Times*, 12 November 1980, p. 125.

Herskovits, Melville J. (1941) 1958. *The Myth of the Negro Past*. Boston: Beacon.

Holt, Grace Sims. 1972a. "Communication in Black Culture: The Other Side of Silence." *Language Research Reports* 6:51–84.

———. 1972b. "Stylin' outta the Black Pulpit." In *Rappin' and Stylin' Out*, edited by Thomas Kochman. Urbana: University of Illinois Press.

Holt, Marie. 1968. "Telling It Like It Is: Southern Style." Xeroxed. Chicago: Northeastern Illinois University, Center for Inner City Studies.

Houston, Susan. 1973. "Black English." *Psychology Today* (March), pp. 45–48.

Hudson, Julius. 1972. "The Hustling Ethic." In *Rappin' and Stylin' Out*, edited by Thomas Kochman. Urbana: University of Illinois Press.

Hymes, Dell. 1972. "Models of the Interaction of Language and Social Life." In *Directions in Sociolinguistics: The Ethnography of Communication*, edited by John J. Gumperz and Dell Hymes. New York: Holt.

Johnson, Kenneth R. 1971. "Black Kinesics: Some Non-verbal Communication Patterns in the Black Culture." *Florida FL Reporter* 9(1–2): 17–20, 57.

————. 1972. "The Vocabulary of Race." In *Rappin' and Stylin' Out*, edited by Thomas Kochman. Urbana: University of Illinois Press.

Keil, Charles. 1966a. "Motion and Feeling in Music." *Journal of Aesthetics and Art Criticism* 24(3): 337–49.

————. 1966b. *Urban Blues*. Chicago: University of Chicago Press.

Keiser, R. Lincoln. 1969. *The Vice Lords: Warriors of the Streets*. New York: Holt.

Kochman, Thomas. 1970. "Toward an Ethnography of Black American Speech Behavior." In *Afro-American Anthropology*, edited by Norman E. Whitten, Jr., and John F. Szwed. New York: Free Press.

————, ed. 1972. *Rappin' and Stylin' Out: Communication in Urban Black America*. Urbana: University of Illinois Press.

Labov, William. 1972a. "The Logic of Non-standard English." In *Language in the Inner City*. Philadelphia: University of Pennsylvania Press.

Labov, William. 1972b. "Rules for Ritual Insults." In *Language in the Inner City*. Philadelphia: University of Pennsylvania Press.

Lamb, Gregory M. 1975. "Will George McGinnis 'tear' up the NBA?" *Christian Science Monitor*, 1 December 1975, p. 36.

Lewis, Diane K. 1975. "The Black Family: Socialization and Sex Roles." *Phylon* 36(3): 221–37.

Liebow, Elliot. 1966. *Tally's Corner*. Boston: Little, Brown.

Marcuse, Herbert. 1969. "Repressive Tolerance." In *A Critique of Pure Tolerance*, edited by Robert Paul Wolff, Barrington Moore, Jr., and Herbert Marcuse. Boston: Beacon.

Maryland, James. 1972. "Shoe-shine on 63rd." In *Rappin' and Stylin' Out*, edited by Thomas Kochman. Urbana: University of Illinois Press.

McDowell, Edwin. 1976. "How Martha Graham Has Influenced Football." *Wall Street Journal,* 20 January 1976, p. 16.

Memmi, Albert. 1965. *The Colonizer and the Colonized.* Boston: Beacon.

Messinger, Sheldon L.; Sampson, Harold; and Towne, Robert T. 1962. "Life as Theatre: Some Notes on the Dramaturgic Approach to Social Reality." *Sociometry* 25:98–110.

Mitchell-Kernan, Claudia. 1971. *Language Behavior in a Black Urban Community.* Monographs of the Language-Behavior Research Laboratory, No. 2. Berkeley: University of California.

"Mr. Trotter and Mr. Wilson." 1915. *Crisis,* January 1915, pp. 119–27.

Murray, Albert. 1971. *The Omni-Americans.* New York: Avon, Discus.

Nilsson, Harry. 1975. "The Flying Saucer Song." In *Sandman.* Sound Recording APLI-1031. Hollywood: RCA.

Ong, Walter J., S.J. 1967. *The Presence of the Word.* New York: Houghton Mifflin, Clarion.

———. 1969. "World as View and World as Event." *American Anthropologist* 71:634–47.

Pateman, Trevor. 1975. *Language, Truth and Politics.* Nottingham: Stroud and Pateman.

Pettigrew, Thomas F. 1964. *A Profile of the Negro American.* Princeton: Van Nostrand Reinhold.

Pierson, Don. 1979. "Henderson's Mouth Puts on Super Show." *Chicago Tribune,* 17 January 1979, Sec. 6, p. 2.

Pryor, Richard. 1979. "Niggers vs. The Police." In *That Nigger's Crazy.* Sound Recording MSK 2287. Berkeley: Stax.

Reisman, Karl. 1974a. "Contrapuntal Conversations in an Antiguan Village." In *Explorations in the Ethnography of Speaking,* edited by Richard Bauman and Joel Sherzer. London: Cambridge University Press.

———. 1974b. "Noise and Order." In *Language in its Social Setting,* edited by William W. Gage. Washington, D.C.: Anthropological Society of Washington.

Rodgers, Carolyn. 1972. "Black Poetry: Where It's At." In *Rappin' and Stylin' Out,* edited by Thomas Kochman. Urbana: University of Illinois Press.

Rosten, Leo. 1970. *The Joys of Yiddish.* New York: Pocket.

Rumill, Ed. 1978. "The Martinet Managers are Tintypes Now." *Christian Science Monitor,* 15 May 1978, p. 16.

Rush, Sheila, and Clark, Christine. 1971. *How to Get Along with Blacks.* New York: Third Press.

Russell, Bill, and Branch, Taylor. 1979. *Second Wind: The Memoirs of an Opinionated Man.* New York: Ballantine.

Saal, Hubert. 1980. "Alvin Ailey's Black Power." *Newsweek,* 29 December 1980, p. 64.

Sahlins, Marshall P., and Service, Elman R. 1960. *Evolution and Culture.* Ann Arbor: University of Michigan Press.

Slater, Philip. 1976. The Pursuit of Loneliness. Rev. ed. Boston: Beacon.

Smitherman, Geneva. 1977. *Talkin and Testifyin: The Language of Black America.* Boston: Houghton Mifflin.

Stewart, William A. 1974. "Acculturative Processes and the Language of the American Negro." In *Language in its Social Setting,* edited by William W. Gage. Washington, D.C.: Anthropological Society of Washington.

Swett, Daniel H. 1969. "Cultural Bias in the American Legal System." *Law and Society Review* 4(1): 79–110.

Townsend, Robert. 1970. *Up the Organization.* New York: Fawcett.

Valentine, Charles A. 1968. *Culture and Poverty.* Chicago: University of Chicago Press.

Wharton, Linda F., and Daniel, Jack L. 1977. "Black Dance: Its African Origins and Continuity." *Minority Voices* 1(2): 73–80.

Wicker, Tom. 1975. *A Time to Die.* New York: Quadrangle.

Williams, Karen. 1976. "Interactional Dynamics in a Girl's Residential School." Xeroxed. Chicago: University of Illinois at Chicago Circle, Department of Communication and Theatre.

Wolf, David. 1972. *Foul!* New York: Warner.

Wolfe, Tom. 1966. "The Nanny Mafia." In *The Kandy-Kolored Tangerine-Flake Streamline Baby.* New York: Pocket.

Young, Bertha. 1967. "Rapping: Man to Woman." Xeroxed. Chicago: Northeastern Illinois University, Center for Inner City Studies.

Index